FIRE and ICE:

Imagination and Intellect in the Catholic Tradition

FIRE and ICE:

Imagination and Intellect in the Catholic Tradition

The 2000 President's Institute on the Catholic
Character at Loyola Marymount University

MARY K. MCCULLOUGH, PH.D., EDITOR

SCRANTON: THE UNIVERSITY OF SCRANTON PRESS

Cover Photography by:
Dave Hill, University Photographer, Loyola Marymount University

"In The Beginning " the stained glass window by Sister Genevieve Underwood, R.S.H.M., which is located in the Center for Prayer and Peace in the Marymount Institute at Loyola Marymount University, has been used for the cover of this book

Library of Congress Cataloging-in-Publication Data

President's Institutes on the Catholic Character of Loyola Marymount University (2000)
  Fire and ice : imagination and intellect in the Catholic tradition : the 2000 President's Institute on the Catholic Character of Loyola Marymount University / Mary K. McCullough, editor.
    p. cm.
  Includes bibliographical references and index.
  ISBN 1-58966-060-9 (hc) -- ISBN 1-58966-058-7 (pbk)
  1. Loyola Marymount University--Congresses. 2. Catholic Church--Education--United States--Congresses. 3. Catholic Church--Doctrines--Congresses.
I. McCullough, Mary K., 1946 - II. Title.

LD3131.L763P74 2003
378.794'94--dc21   2003054153

Distribution:

University of Scranton Press
Chicago Distribution Center
11030 S. Langley
Chicago IL 60628

PRINTED IN THE UNITED STATES OF AMERICA

Dedication

To gifts of imagination and intellect
To gifts of life and light: Kevin, Amy, Justin,
and Tanya

Special thanks to: Annette and Becky

CONTENTS

FOREWORD

Catholic Character in Context:
The President's Institute at Loyola Marymount University

Robert V. Caro, S.J.

During the 1999–2000 academic year I was chair of Loyola Marymount University's Committee on Mission and Identity. In that role I was privileged to serve as program coordinator for the President's Institute on the Catholic Character of the University, which took place May 15–19, 2000.

It was the fifth in the series of Institutes inaugurated in 1996 by President Thomas P. O'Malley, S.J. From the beginning, the yearly Institutes were envisioned as weeklong seminars for groups of up to 20 tenured and tenure-track faculty. Participants committed themselves to serious background reading, attendance at presentations by distinguished speakers from on and off campus, small-group breakout sessions, and ongoing sharing across disciplines during meals, prayer, and moments of reflection. During the summer months following the Institute, participants responded in writing to what they had learned.

Previous Institutes typically highlighted characteristic emphases of LMU's founding religious orders, the Society of Jesus and the Religious of the Sacred Heart of Mary. In 1998, for example, the theme was *Faith Doing Justice*; in 1999, *Finding God in All Things*. Sonnets by Jesuit poet Gerard Manley Hopkins provided epigraphs for these two Institutes, and background readings included excerpts from official documents of the two religious orders. For Institute 2000, however, the planning committee decided to focus more broadly on the underlying Catholic vision that distinguishes Loyola Marymount from its secular counterparts and even from religiously affiliated schools of other Christian traditions. The theme agreed upon was "Fire and Ice: Imagination and Intellect in the Catholic Tradition." The background readings included selections from the 1998 study by James Burtchaell, C.S.C., *The Dying of the Light: The Disengagement of Colleges and Universities from Their*

Christian Churches. The point of including the Burtchaell piece was not to affirm his gloomy predictions but by reverse suggestion to underscore the importance of the intellectual and imaginative tradition that is Loyola Marymount's birthright as a Catholic university. The Burtchaell piece also served to highlight the significance on Catholic campuses of programs like the President's Institute as a way of counteracting the drift toward secularization.

The present volume gathers together the Institute's five major presentations, as well as six response papers that explore connections between Institute themes and the writers' disciplines or, more broadly, their experience as faculty members at LMU.

In his keynote presentation on the opening day of the Institute, Michael Engh, S.J., Associate Professor of History at Loyola Marymount, traced the University's evolution from a custodial model of Catholic higher education to an empowerment model, challenging his colleagues to involve themselves in scripting the future of "the intellectual and imaginative life of the Catholic university" (Engh, 2003, p.21). Their greatest contribution, he said, will be to do what faculty does best:

> . . . to enliven minds and to quicken spirits, to inspire a love of learning and a pursuit of virtue, and to enkindle a curiosity about the many faces and forms of Truth. By educating well [he concluded], we incarnate anew the intellectual heritage that distinguishes this University and links us to Gailhac, Cure Pélissier [Father John Gailhac and Mother St. Jean Cure Pélissier were the founders in 1849 of the Religious of the Sacred Heart of Mary.] and Loyola, to Aquinas and Augustine, and to the Word first spoken by the Divine in our human history. (p. 21)

While Engh concluded with the hopeful vision of a faculty who will incarnate anew Loyola Marymount's intellectual heritage, Dr. Robert Bellah's presentation the following day, "On Being Catholic and American," was insistent that a university's Catholic identity is not possible without genuinely Catholic scholars. The distinguished Emeritus Professor of the Sociology of Religion from the University of California at Berkeley put the matter this way: "Only the presence of a number of scholars who exemplify the commitment to Catholic identity in dialogue with the modern world will make the project of an American Catholic university viable today" (Bellah, 2003, p. 43).

Bellah's magisterial address sketched the waves of modernity that have confronted the Church since the Protestant Reformation. Borrowing and developing David Tracy's distinction between the dialectical and analogical imagination (characteristic respectively of Protestant and Catholic theology), he went on to argue that American Catholics ". . . have imbibed more Protestantism than they might be aware of, because American culture and American academic culture in particular, are Protestant to the bone" (p. 40). Yet, he said, "It is my belief that this is a Catholic moment in American cultural history and that Protestants and Catholics alike badly need an infusion of the analogical imagination to help us overcome the cultural confusion into which we have fallen" (p. 40). Bellah instanced Charles Taylor and Alasdair MacIntyre as examples of scholars whose Catholic substance might speak to the confusions of post-modernity. He saw them as ". . . role models for the kind of faculty members who could make a university with a Catholic identity become a reality today" (p. 41). Bellah acknowledged that it is not an easy task to recruit and hire such scholars, but he also warned that, "No amount of gimmicks can substitute for the presence of [genuine Catholic scholars]" (p. 43).

Like Bellah, Dr. Doris Donnelly, Professor of Theology at John Carroll University in Cleveland and Institute presenter, invoked David Tracy's distinction between the dialectical and analogical imagination. Her particular concern was with the analogical imagination and its implications for sacramental theology. She pointed to a post-Vatican II understanding that encompasses more than the seven particular sacraments in a ". . . heightened awareness of the strength of [many] signs to disclose the beyond" (Donnelly, 2003, p. 52). According to Donnelly,

> What often helps the eventual progressive disclosure of sacramental symbolism is familiarity with the world outside the official religious sphere—for example, in the arts—in poetry, music, and painting—in subjects we teach, in issues we raise in the classroom, and the discoveries we make there as well. Sometimes, and maybe it is most often, those signs of grace, of God's presence in the world, are found in the ordinary. (pp. 52–53)

Donnelly went on to cite three contemporary writers—Kathleen Norris, Brian Doyle, and Anne Sexton—whom she sees as having this gift of finding God in the ordinary and whose work presents a

> "challenge for educators . . . to offer a contemplative perspective—a pause from accumulation [of information] to simplicity—an invitation to slow down and allow what lies before [their students] to disclose all that is there beyond the surface if they (and we) would only take time to notice" (p. 54).

Exemplary teacher that she is, Donnelly gave Institute participants the "homework" assignment of writing a poem during the afternoon reading period. It was a daunting challenge, but most accepted it. They were pleased to share their results with the group, and Donnelly has appended five of the poems to the printed version of her presentation. The poems serve to illustrate the analogical or sacramental imagination at work and nicely confirm Donnelly's suggestions about the evocative power of metaphor and symbol to reveal the presence of God in the ordinary events of daily life.

Richard Blake, S.J., Professor of Film Studies at Boston College and film critic for *America* magazine, developed his Institute presentation in two parts: "Woody Allen: God as Jewish Mother" and "Francis Coppola: Baptism by Fire and Water." His purpose was to illustrate, through generous film clips, commentary, and discussion, the distinctively Jewish and Catholic sensibilities that inform the work of the two cinema artists. The written version of Blake's presentation, subtitled "Religious Roots of Coppola's Vietnam Epic," focuses on the script development of *Apocalypse Now.* It develops the thesis that Coppola "was guided, consciously or not, by a particularly Catholic way of interpreting the moral universe in which his characters seek some form of redemption" (Blake, 2003, p. 67). Blake makes his point through a careful analysis of Coppola's rewriting of John Milius's 1969 *Apocalypse* script. The analysis demonstrates that Coppola brought the final film version much closer to its roots in Joseph Conrad's *Heart of Darkness*—which is not surprising, since ". . . through their [Catholic] roots the two artists [Coppola and Conrad] show a remarkable affinity" (p. 67). Blake draws out parallels between Marlow (in the novel) and Willard (in the film), showing how both characters grapple with the dynamics of salvation and move from their experience of the dark world of sin to reinsertion in the communion of civilization. His study is thus a powerful, even startling, exposition of the Catholic imagination and of the hope held out by its underlying worldview.

Of course not all faculty members know this underlying worldview from inside the faith community. This fact prompted University President Robert B. Lawton, S.J., to focus his concluding presentation during the weeklong Institute, on the important contributions of non-Catholics to Loyola Marymount's academic life. Entitled "The Modern Catholic University: How Far from Eden?", his remarks called into question the idea of a paradisiacal past from which universities like Loyola Marymount have been exiled—or to which they should return by becoming "entirely or overwhelmingly Catholic in [their] faculty, staff, and students" (Lawton, 2003, p. 89). In rejecting such a purist view of religiously affiliated higher education, the president seemed to opt instead for a model that in some respects approaches Robert Benne's "intentionally pluralist" category (Benne, 2001, p. 49). According to Lawton:

> Those of us who are Catholic benefit enormously from the presence of people whose ways of viewing God and the world are far different from our own. Such people question our clichés, shake our categories, stretch our imaginations and touch our hearts. God is far too big, God's world far too intricately textured, to be exhausted by the insights of any one tradition, religious or intellectual, or even by the sum of all traditions. (p. 91)

Lawton's remarks struck a responsive chord with Institute participants, pointing as they did to a style of religious identity marked by an ecumenical and interreligious openness. In other words, in his view, Loyola Marymount should be a Catholic university with both a large C and a small c—cherishing, developing, and handing on its distinctive Catholic intellectual and imaginative tradition, but at the same time valuing the interplay of honest dialogue between that tradition and other ways of seeking truth.

Institute participants were unanimous in applauding Lawton's inclusive, optimistic perspective, a reaction that paralleled their enthusiasm for Engh's opening-day evocation of LMU's history. As one participant remarked in the anonymous evaluations at the end of the week, Engh enabled the group to see their own careers ". . . as a piece in a much bigger picture." More challenging, however, were the three midweek presentations by Bellah, Donnelly, and Blake, treating, as they did, certain philosophical and theological underpinnings of the Catholic intellectual/imaginative traditions. Understandably, some faculty, not attuned to those traditions, were initially puzzled when they found themselves encountering distinctions between analogical and dialectical reasoning, notions of theological anthropology, or the implications of the Incarnation for a sacramental view of the world. Still, the three presenters convincingly explored important aspects of the intellectual and imaginative heritage that should help shape a Catholic university, and each of them, whether for style or content or both, found champions among the participants. In the words of one faculty member, which easily might have been echoed by the group, the experience of the Institute was ". . . an amazing opportunity to rethink many key issues in my life."

This statement is a fitting tribute to the success of the Institute in challenging faculty to a new awareness of the Catholic character of Loyola Marymount. Yet beyond heightened awareness or deepened appreciation, participants were asked to submit papers in which they responded in practical ways to Institute-related themes. Six of these papers have been selected for inclusion in this volume. Several take the form of academic essays that draw on themes from the Institute as hermeneutic principles. Others are in the nature of personal reflections on the authors' experiences as faculty members, while still others seem to combine elements of both approaches. The papers are an eclectic mix, but each in its own way reflects an effort to explore the practical implications of the Institute in the ongoing life and work of faculty members.

Scott Wood, Associate Clinical Professor in the law school, finds his inspiration in both a whimsical poem by W.H. Auden, "Law Like Love," and Bellah's urging of the use of metanarratives—the analogical reading of texts—to engage students' imaginations. Wood is primarily concerned with law students' imaginations, and the literary texts he chooses to analyze are, appropriately, "The Eumenides" from Aeschylus' *Oresteia* trilogy and Shakespeare's *Measure for Measure*. "Can these imaginative artifacts of legal process," he asks, "be read analogically to produce metanarratives? And do any such metanarratives show that law is like love in ways that make sense, even to those inclined to regard the law in purely instrumental terms?" (Wood, 2003, p. 97). His careful study yields the conclusion that in Aeschylus' Athens, no less than in Shakespeare's Vienna, the rule of revenge is ". . . subsumed into a judicial system based on the complex interplay of law and mercy" (p. 107). Thus, law *is* like love. Wood insists that his experience in teaching literature to law students validates this striking simile:

> As we explore the literary analogies, [students] begin to see beyond the instrumental purposes of law to engage a larger, more complicated vision. As they report on the "aptness of unexpected resemblance," on the connections between law as pronounced and law as lived, they consistently draw insight from themselves and each other. Together they find, through the literature, a greater sense of who they are and what their life in law might be: imagining justice. (p. 108)

Sharon Locy, Professor of English, presents a study of what she calls "catastrophic grace" (Locy, 2003, p. 111) in three short stories by Flannery O'Connor. Her paper draws its framework of interpretation from themes suggested by the Institute. Much as Blake's keynote presentation explored the moral universe of *Apocalypse Now*, Locy explores the moral universe of the protagonists in "A Good Man Is Hard to Find," "Everything That Rises Must Converge," and "Revelation"—stories that she believes cannot be adequately understood ". . . without attention to O'Connor's development of them as sacramental, particularly as analogues for the sacrament of penance" (p. 111). Responding to ideas suggested by both Bellah and Donnelly, Locy moves beyond the familiar interpretation of O'Connor's work as reflecting the breakthrough of God's grace in bizarre and startling events. In the three protagonists' inchoate examinations of conscience, acknowledgement of sin, or acceptance of a life of repentance, she finds—in decidedly nonritual contexts—very basic elements of the sacrament of Penance. She thus suggests, without saying so explicitly, that the sacramental principle is itself analogous. Thus, for Locy, the sacrament of Penance becomes the outward sign or ratification of God's grace already at work in breakthrough moments of repentance—moments that can occur in everyday life, sometimes induced in quite shocking ways.

In "The Flesh of Adam: Women, Bodies, and the Sacramental Imagination," Marie Anne Mayeski, Professor of Historical Theology, offers a fresh analysis of two medieval women writers, Dhuoda of Septimania and Julian of Norwich. Her purpose is to show how each moved away from the body-soul dualism characteristic of much of the Christian thought in their centuries. The mystery of the Incarnation as the primordial sacrament—God's Word becoming flesh—is at the heart of this study that underscores the idea that ". . . all human embodiment is a sacred reality" (Mayeski, 2003, p. 128). While the approaches of the two medieval writers differ, the texts of both converge on the idea that the human body is the ". . . irreplaceable reality that establishes the identity between Adam, Christ and all of humanity" (p. 137). Mayeski concludes her careful study on a note of contemporary pedagogical relevance. She writes:

> We live in a world that swings drunkenly between exploitation and repression in its understanding of human embodiment, with Catholic Christianity perceived to be firmly on the side of repression. Julian and Dhuoda point to an alternative way of understanding the body's full symbolic significance, a way consistent with the enduring Catholic tradition of sacramental imagination. These texts—and others like them—may not, in themselves, change the Catholic theological world. But in the curriculum of a Catholic university they can serve to enliven a sacramental imagination and hold the Christian paradox at the center of our attention. (p. 138)

Howard Lavick, Associate Professor of Film and Television, offers a brief but insightful paper sparked by ideas drawn from background reading for Donnelly's keynote presentation. His essay is an exploration of parallels between faith communities and the media in the way both rely on image and metaphor/symbol to convey meaning—meaning that speaks to the heart as well as the head. He points out that the difference between looking and seeing, between hearing and listening, between knowing and believing ". . . is the chasm between intellect and imagination" (Lavick, 2003, p. 143). And, whether in church or synagogue, whether in film or television, if the chasm is not bridged, ". . . if the message is not seen or heard or believed—then how is the soul to be touched, the lesson learned?"

Stephanie August is Assistant Professor of Computer Science and Electrical Engineering. She participated in the President's Institute at the end of her first year as a tenure-track faculty member and found the week a challenging experience—one that prompted her ". . . to reconsider . . . the way my faith affects my interactions with students, and ultimately the way commitment to mission transforms and influences my approach to teaching computer science" (August, 2003, p. 145). August invokes insights from both Donnelly and Bellah (among others) to argue that Catholic education is about making connections. Donnelly helped her to realize, for example, that it is not difficult to find God in the banal logic of a computer program. Bellah underscored for her the idea that true scholars—including computer scientists—must be knowledgeable or skillful in their disciplines, as well as persons of conscience and strong character. The ultimate connection for August, as she looks around at students in her computer lab, is between an imagination alive with the excitement of new ideas, and a willingness to temper that excitement with the colder calculations of reason. "In the final analysis," she suggests, "it is not just the fire of imagination or the ice of intellect, it is the way the two work in communion with each other" (p. 151) that leads to new discoveries of how God's creation unfolds and how to build his kingdom on earth.

Unlike August, Michael Geis, Professor of Chemistry and Biochemistry, writes from the perspective of a longtime faculty member at Loyola Marymount who is also an alumnus (Class of '62). He compares the mission statement from that earlier era with the current version and concludes that the University's fundamental purpose remains intact. Nonetheless, he acknowledges ". . . enough significant change" (Geis, 2003 p. 157) at LMU and other universities like it to urge them to consider seriously ". . . what they are and what they are becoming" (p. 157). Beginning with a 1989 national gathering at Georgetown, Geis traces the history of conferences, and other initiatives during the 1990s, that brought together Jesuits and their co-workers to explore the nature of the modern Jesuit university. The Lilly Network of Church-Related Colleges and Universities was engaged in a parallel enterprise, and on both fronts the conclusion was the same: that at religiously affiliated schools a critical mass of faculty sympathetic to their history and nature is ". . . essential for maintaining their intellectual, ethical, and religious characteristics" (p. 158). This points, of course, toward efforts to hire for mission, which

Geis, with Bellah, sees as the key challenge that LMU and other Catholic colleges and universities must confront at the beginning of the twenty-first century.

The eleven papers gathered together in this volume make a modest contribution to an ongoing conversation and a growing body of literature on the intellectual and imaginative vision that distinguishes Catholic higher education. May their publication extend to interested audiences beyond Loyola Marymount's campus the stimulating insights of five keynote presenters and the thoughtful responses of six faculty participants at the 2000 President's Institute.

As program coordinator for that Institute, I wish to note with gratitude a Lilly Fellows Mentoring Grant that helped to make it—and this volume—possible.

REFERENCES

August, S. E. (2003). "Computer Science, Community, and Faith." In M. K. McCullough (Ed.), *Fire and Ice: Imagination and Intellect in the Catholic Tradition* (pp. 145–152). Scranton, PA: University of Scranton Press.

Bellah, R. N. (2003). "On Being Catholic and American." In M. K. McCullough (Ed.), *Fire and Ice: Imagination and Intellect in the Catholic Tradition* (pp. 31–48). Scranton, PA: University of Scranton Press.

Benne, R. (2001). *Quality With Soul: How Six Premier Colleges and Universities Keep Faith With Their Religious Traditions.* Grand Rapids: Eerdmans.

Blake, R., S.J. (2003). "The Genesis of Apocalypse: Religious Roots of Coppola's Vietnam Epic." In M. K. McCullough (Ed.), *Fire and Ice: Imagination and Intellect in the Catholic Tradition* (pp. 67–87). Scranton, PA: University of Scranton Press.

Donnelly, D., (2003). "The Catholic Sacramental Imagination." In M. K. McCullough (Ed.), *Fire and Ice: Imagination and Intellect in the Catholic Tradition* (pp. 49–66). Scranton, PA: University of Scranton Press.

Engh, M. E., S.J. (2003). "The Best Sort of Liberal Education: A History of the Intellectual Tradition at Loyola Marymount University." In M. K. McCullough (Ed.), *Fire and Ice: Imagination and Intellect in the Catholic Tradition* (pp. 1–29). Scranton, PA: University of Scranton Press.

Geis, M. P. (2003). A Twenty-First Century Challenge: Hiring for Mission in Catholic Higher Education. In M. K. McCullough (Ed.), *Fire and Ice: Imagination and Intellect in the Catholic Tradition* (pp. 153–161). Scranton, PA: University of Scranton Press.

Lavick, H. (2003). "Believing Is Seeing: *Field of Dreams* as Liturgy?" In M. K. McCullough (Ed.), *Fire and Ice: Imagination and Intellect in the Catholic Tradition* (pp. 39–144). Scranton, PA: University of Scranton Press.

Lawton, R. B., S.J. (2003). "The Modern Catholic University: How Far from Eden?" In M. K. McCullough (Ed.), *Fire and Ice: Imagination and Intellect in the Catholic Tradition* (pp. 89–93). Scranton, PA: University of Scranton Press.

Locy, S. (2003). "Catastrophic Grace: Flannery O'Connor and the Catholic Imagination." In M. K. McCullough (Ed.), *Fire and Ice: Imagination and Intellect in the Catholic Tradition* (pp. 111–125). Scranton, PA: University of Scranton Press.

Mayeski, M. A. (2003). "The Flesh of Adam: Women, Bodies, and the Sacramental Imagination." In M. K. McCullough (Ed.), *Fire and Ice: Imagination and Intellect in the Catholic Tradition* (pp. 127–138). Scranton, PA: University of Scranton Press.

Wood, S. (2003). Imagining Justice: Is Law Like Love?" In M. K. McCullough (Ed.), *Fire and Ice: Imagination and Intellect in the Catholic Tradition* (pp. 95–109). Scranton, PA: University of Scranton Press.

PART I

Intellect and Imagination in the Catholic Tradition

The Best Sort of Liberal Education:
A History of the Intellectual Tradition at
Loyola Marymount University

Michael E. Engh, S.J.

In his widely recognized book, *Lives on the Boundary* (1989), learning expert Mike Rose maintains that he received ". . . the best sort of liberal education" while an undergraduate at Loyola University of Los Angeles, 1961–1965. Rose marvels that he attended a school conscious of its place in the centuries-old Christian practice of linking imagination, learning, and religious belief. He praises his professors for their courses in poetry, drama, philosophy, and theology which awakened in students the awareness of the creativity and depth of the human mind. Besides outstanding instruction, Rose also benefited from the teachers' excitement about learning and their encouragement to develop his full potential. His heroes are still instructors like Frank Carothers, the late Ted Erlandson, and Reverend Clint Alberston, S.J., who guided him toward discoveries with life-changing consequences.

The all-male school that Mike Rose remembers so fondly no longer exists. Loyola University and Marymount College merged to form the coeducational Loyola Marymount University (LMU) in 1973. Painful upheavals rocked American society in the 1960s and 1970s and altered the curriculum and governance of all institutions of higher education. At the same time, the Roman Catholic Church initiated widespread reform that reverberated throughout religious orders such as LMU's founding religious communities, the Religious of the Sacred Heart of Mary (the Marymount Sisters) and the Society of Jesus (the Jesuits). The impact of combined religious and social changes transformed Catholic higher education so thoroughly that the defining characteristics of schools like LMU were frequently obscured or even eclipsed. Their histories, traditions, and educational philosophies were often neglected, forgotten, or simply no longer explained.

As members of the present faculty, we live with the consequences of these developments of the past 30 years. The numbers of

1

religious personnel in the classroom have declined over these decades, and our courses differ markedly from the strict core curriculum Mike Rose knew. We stand, however, in the tradition of the professors Rose cherished who opened to him the world of the intellect. We inherit from them a legacy rooted in imagination and in religious faith, dedicated to serious scholarship, and committed to educating the whole person. As recipients of this heritage, we willy-nilly find ourselves bequeathed important responsibilities. How well we understand our origins and our predecessors' actions will affect how generously we serve the school, as well as how we influence the decisions of what kind of university we want to create.

I. The Christian Tradition of Universities and Loyola Marymount University

Universities as we know them originated in western Europe under the patronage and support of the Roman Catholic Church. The tradition of *fides quarens intellectum*—faith seeking understanding— dates back even further to the first centuries of the Christian era. Philosophers and theologians wrestled with reconciling Christian beliefs with their contemporary understandings of human nature, the purpose and goals of human existence, and the principles needed for virtue and a good life. Augustine of Hippo and Thomas Aquinas, for example, noted that human truth mirrors the divine Truth. Given this divine origin, nothing in the created world should escape human notice; all was worthy of examination and study. From monasteries to cathedral schools, learning became an essential component of Christian activity in society.

In the medieval era, the Catholic Church promoted universities for the pursuit of a higher education that culminated in the study of theology, the "queen of the sciences." Such schools required the mastery of the preparatory courses of the *trivium* and *quadrivium*, the humane or liberal studies, for other advanced degrees in philosophy, law, and medicine. The University of Paris refined the sequencing of studies, and, during the high Renaissance, it was there that Ignatius Loyola enrolled, matriculated, and took his Master's degree in theology. Amongst the students he met, Ignatius drew together a group of men who eventually formed a Society of Jesus and sought some means to serve the needs of the Church.

Ignatius deeply appreciated the humanistic studies that he and his companions completed in Paris, yet his was a spiritual humanism informed by the insights he had gained through his spiritual experiences. Ignatius found that God was both present and active in the world, so that the universe was never merely secular or profane. The divine spark glowed in all created things and burned most brightly in human beings and in their imagination and intellect. In a spirituality that was both worldly and humanistic, Ignatius spoke of "finding God in all things." He discovered God incarnated in the world, immersed in all creation, and alive in all human endeavors for the good (Modras, 1995). Ignatius developed his insights in two volumes that form the heart of Jesuit spirituality and learning: the slim tome of the *Spiritual Exercises* and a heftier book, the *Constitutions of the Society of Jesus* (Ganss, 1992).

Pope Paul III dispatched these educated priests to lecture at the University of Rome, the University of Mainz, and at Ingolstadt (O'Malley, 1993). Ignatius also desired that new members of the religious order be well educated, so he established houses or "colleges" attached to universities in the Italian states, in Spain, and in Portugal (Lucas, 2000). These academic residences attracted the notice of parents who valued the Renaissance course of studies, and they approached Ignatius to educate their sons alongside the Jesuit seminarians (known as scholastics). By agreeing, Ignatius commenced the Jesuit engagement in the formal education of the Catholic laity that continues to the present. The rapid success of these Jesuit schools was due, in large part, to the pedagogy they formulated:

> As was often true with other endeavors, the Jesuits created relatively few of the components of their educational program, but they put those parts together in a way and on a scale that had never been done before. It was the combination, not any single feature, that distinguished the education offered in the Jesuit schools from what was offered elsewhere. (O'Malley, 1993, p. 225)

In particular, the curriculum emphasized character formation, provided sequential learning of subjects based on mastery of material, and included a simple religious program that encouraged a personal appropriation of religious and ethical values (Atterbury, personal interview, 1999; Russell, personal interview, 1999). Most importantly, the Jesuits emphasized the importance of loving the students and knowing them as individuals (O'Malley, 1993).

Jesuits developed and revised these principles, which they finally published in 1599 as the *Ratio Studiorum* ("plan of studies"). As historian John O'Malley, S.J., has observed, "The *Ratio* assumed that literary or humanistic studies could be integrated with the study of professional or scientific subjects . . . that the humanistic program of the Renaissance was compatible with the Scholastic program of the Middle Ages" (O'Malley, 1999). With this guidebook in hand, Jesuits, by 1773, founded schools that numbered over 800, including colleges, universities, boarding schools, and seminaries and enrolled approximately 200,000 students in Europe, Asia, and the Americas. In that year, however, the Holy See suppressed the Society of Jesus, and all but 13 schools were lost to the order (Codina, 2000). Empress Catherine the Great of Russia refused to implement the papal decree, so a small cadre of Jesuits survived in her empire and formed the nucleus for a revival of the order in 1814. The Jesuit return on a world-wide basis in the 19th century coincided with significant religious developments elsewhere in Europe.

In southeastern France, Reverend John Gailhac and Mother St. John Cure-Pelissier founded the Religious of the Sacred Heart of Mary in 1849, in the midst of the Catholic revival that swept the nation at the conclusion of the Napoleonic wars. Gailhac began several works for the needy in the city of Beziers, and Pelissier headed a group of women who shared her vision of serving poor women and abandoned children (Do Campo Sampaio, 1990). They encouraged the sisters to "know and to love God" and to undertake any ministry that would make God known and loved by others. They urged the sisters to study the needs of any land where they worked and to respond in whatever way they could to meet those needs, according to the sisters' talents and abilities (Bailey & McMahaon, 1999; Gussenhoven, 1985; Kearney, 1965). Like so many women's religious orders of that era, the Religious of the Sacred Heart of Mary identified education as one of the preeminent needs of the Church.

When invited to open schools in the United States, Gailhac recommended a course of studies that would develop both knowledge (science) and piety (piete) so that virtue provided a foundation for learning. The first "Marymount" Sisters in the United States carried the principles that would link their educational system to the wider tradition of Catholic schooling in the post-Reformation era. They advocated the care and concern for the total growth of the individual, a liberal arts education, and a respect for all cultures by means of international education. On the recommendation of Pope Pius IX, Gailhac missioned six Sisters to establish an academy in the United States, which opened in Sag Harbor, Long Island in 1877 (Connell, 1993). From there the Sisters established other schools on Long Island, in the Bronx, and in Tarrytown-on-Hudson in Westchester County.

Marymount College opened at Tarrytown in 1918 under the leadership of Mother Joseph Butler, R.S.H.M., and soon received accreditation from the state of New York. Like the Jesuits, the Religious of the Sacred Heart of Mary in the United States discovered a deep antipathy towards Roman Catholicism. Further, the Sisters and the Jesuits encountered an educational establishment that was thoroughly Protestant in its origins, expressions, and values. Because of this widespread hostility towards their church, Catholic bishops, religious, and laity recognized the need for private and parochial education to assure the survival of their faith in the United States.

American universities and colleges had begun as religiously inspired and administered institutions where Protestant Christianity trained its ministers as well as lawyers, doctors, bankers, and other professionals (Marsden, 1994). The vast majority of 18th and 19th century educators held that to be American was to be Protestant, one who believed in the ideals of "freedom, democracy, benevolence, justice, reform, inclusiveness, brotherhood, and service." These educators further assumed that Roman Catholicism was the source of absolutism and of blind obedience. Thus the term, "Catholic university," was an oxymoron (Marsden, 1994).

The founders and later administrators of the nation's colleges worked closely with public officials in extending the "free" or public school throughout the United States in the 19th century. These grammar schools were open to all citizens, but a Protestant ethos pervaded the classroom, from opening prayers and reading from the King James version of the Bible, to textbooks which denigrated Catholic countries, their governments and culture, as well as the Catholic Church itself. When Catholic immigrants began arriving in large numbers in the 1840s and 1850s, Catholic parents, parish priests, and bishops noisily challenged the Protestant hegemony in education.

The resulting conflicts led to "school wars" and anti-Catholic riots in cities such as Boston, Philadelphia, and New York (Morris, 1997; Ravitch, 1974). Catholic leaders reacted by constructing a separate world of institutions to protect the faith of the immigrant. Parochial schools, high schools, colleges, orphanages, hospitals, homes for the aged, and parish churches provided a safe haven from the threats to their religious sensibilities (Gleason, 1995; McKevitt, 1991). Bishops manifested a "custodial approach" towards parishioners and argued that "the Faith" could best be "preserved" if Catholics were educated separately from a highly suspect Protestant society (Dolan, 1985). This view extended to professional training as well, and required Catholic schools of law, medicine, dentistry, education, and social work. Graduates of these institutions formed Catholic professional associations, such as the American Catholic Historical Association, where they could discuss issues in an atmosphere that was more congenial—"safer" for the Faith—than that found in secular societies (Gleason, 1987).

II. The Early Years at Loyola Marymount University

The prevailing "custodial" approach to the laity marked the thinking both of the Jesuit and Marymount superiors when they were asked to open schools in southern California. The respective predecessor institutions of the University were Los Angeles College, which opened inauspiciously in 1911, and Marymount School, which first received students in 1923. The Irish-born bishop of the diocese in 1911, Thomas J. Conaty, was a graduate of the Jesuits' College of the Holy Cross (Worchester, MA) and had served as the less-than-successful second president of the Catholic University of America in Washington, D.C. He desired a Catholic college in Los Angeles to offer professional training, such as in law, but he discovered that the administrators of the existing Catholic institution, St. Vincent's College, were not interested in his plans. When pressured by the bishop, the Vincentian Fathers rather abruptly withdrew, and six Jesuits (two priests and four scholastics) opened a new school, Los Angeles College, in the fall of 1911 (*First Annual Catalogue of Los Angeles College*, 1911; Weber, 1970). Beginning as a high school, the first year of college-level courses was not offered until the fall of 1914. In each of the next three academic terms another year of study was offered until a four-year collegiate curriculum was in place by the fall of 1917.

The Jesuits obtained a state charter in 1918 and renamed the school Loyola College, in honor of the founder of their order, St. Ignatius Loyola. Two years later they opened the school of law that Conaty had so desired, and classes met in the evenings, from 7:30 to 9:30, four nights per week. (First known as St. Vincent's School of Law, the name later changed to Loyola Law School.) Undergraduates of the college were entitled to enroll in law school classes in those years. It is important to note two other features about the enrollment that distinguished the law school for its time and place. School records and yearbooks clearly document that women enrolled in the first year, received degrees, and even had their own sorority (*Rho Mu Phi*). A strong oral tradition also maintains that Loyola was the first law school in Los Angeles to admit Jewish students. Jews faced exclusion not only from local law schools, but also from country clubs, and from the city's elite social institutions, such as the Jonathan Club and the California Club (Bradshaw, 1972; Engh, 2000; Vorspan & Gartner, 1970).

A little over a mile to the south of the Jesuit school on Venice Boulevard at Normandie, the Marymount Sisters opened their school, "Marymount-in-the-West," in September, 1923. Conaty's successor, Bishop John J. Cantwell, had written the year previously to Tarrytown, New York, and pleaded for Sisters to teach the daughters of the Catholic elite, whom he termed "poor little rich children." Cantwell feared that, "Unless something can be done the leaders in Catholic society in this city in years to come will be tainted with Protestantism, and our marriages among the well-to-do classes will be largely mixed" (Cantwell, 1922). Led by one of the Marymount College faculty members, Mother Cecilia Rafter, R.S.H.M., seven Sisters opened the school in a rented house, the Brockman Estate, at 814 West 28th Street.

On the first day of classes, the Sisters welcomed five students, who ranged from first grade through the junior year of high school; on the second day, two more students arrived. Enrollment steadily increased, and in time the estate teemed with several dozen elementary and secondary students. In these early years, the school functioned as a branch of Marymount College in Tarrytown, New York. In 1928, growth in enrollment to sixty students, expansion of the curriculum, and accreditation by the University of California prompted the Sisters to plan to secure a new site for the school. They decided upon

Westwood, and in 1931 Marymount School relocated to Sunset Boulevard, on the north side of the then-new U.C.L.A. campus. Two years
later, the Junior College opened on that campus to accommodate the
growing demand for the education that the Sisters offered (Kearney,
1965).

Loyola also grew and expanded its curriculum to include new
schools of Commerce and Engineering. In 1926, Father Joseph
Sullivan, S.J., assumed the leadership of Loyola College, immediately
planned a major fund drive, and created a Board of Regents that
counted some of the most powerful men in the city and, significantly,
included Protestants and Jews. The developer of Playa del Rey, Fritz B.
Burns, introduced Sullivan to another developer, Harry Culver, and persuaded Culver to give the Jesuits 100 acres in the Del Rey hills
(Hannon, personal interview, 1997). Sullivan switched the object of the
fund drive from new buildings on Venice Boulevard to a new $20 mil-
lion campus on the west side of the city. Sullivan broke ground on what
we now know as the Westchester campus in May 1928, in the presence
of 10,000 spectators. Three buildings quickly appeared: St. Robert's
Hall, Xavier Hall (a residence for faculty and students), and the locker
room for athletics (torn down in the summer of 1999). The great
Depression intervened to forestall further construction and to defer the
full realization of Sullivan's dreams.

In the area of the creative arts, the catalogues reveal a fixed
curriculum with little flexibility, few electives, and set classes. Nonetheless, a Music Department began offering classes in choir, band, and
orchestra in 1923, though course credit did not come until 1934. These
offerings expanded to include a Radio Department (for radio reading,
writing, and drama) in 1938. The Del Rey Players organized in 1934 to
present amateur theatre productions. The school sponsored visiting
speakers, such as G. K. Chesterton, who lectured in 1931 at the Phil-
harmonic Auditorium. The educational goals of the early years appear
clearly in a statement that appeared for many years in the school bulletin and described "the Loyola Man":

> Loyola aims to train a man for success and for possible
> greatness; but whatever a man's worldly achievement,
> Loyola's training insists that his design of living include
> the fulfillment of his obligations toward God and his own
> soul, prepares him to be, in the best sense, a Complete an,
> a Citizen of Two Worlds. (*Loyola University Bulletin*,
> 1947)

The Sisters at Marymount College shared similar, though gender-specific, goals for the students they taught. They strove to ". . . give their pupils an education, moral, physical, and intellectual, which will enable them to be, throughout their lives, models of every virtue and useful and accomplished members of society" (*Marymount School Catalogue*, 1936). The curriculum emphasized the role that women played in society, an understanding and appreciation of the arts, an intellectualism of thinking critically and creatively, and a realization of the fundamental spiritual values of life. The Sisters desired that ultimately each young woman achieve a "harmony of mind and soul and body."

These statements of educational philosophy, in the catalogues of both schools, strongly emphasized the necessity of religious training as part of the collegiate preparation for life after graduation. At both schools, the custodial approach to Catholic education remained strong into the 1960s. Marymount's emphasis on the arts surpassed Loyola's, though the men's college annually staged operettas, concerts, and plays at venues such as the Wilshire Ebell theatre. Much of the Marymount curriculum reflected the conservative Catholic definition of that time which limited women's roles to wife, mother, or religious. The difference was an emphasis on advanced education and refinement.

Both schools changed dramatically after World War II in both enrollment and curriculum. Returning veterans took advantage of the G.I. Bill and boosted enrollment at Loyola to 1500 students by 1948. Marymount began four-year collegiate instruction that same year to accommodate demand from a burgeoning Catholic population. Both schools expanded their offerings of courses and departments. Marymount's catalogue for 1949–50 listed departments of music, art, theatre arts, and radio. By 1951, art expanded to include painting, advertising art, interior design, and costume design. At Loyola, a drama department augmented the music (principally for the band and glee club) and radio departments in 1947, as did, briefly, a communication arts department, from 1950 to 1952 (*Bulletin*, 1947, 1948).

The murder of an African-American family in Fontana in 1945 outraged one member of Loyola's faculty, Reverend George Dunne, S.J., of the political science department. Using imagination to voice his passion for justice, he wrote a two-act play, *Trial by Fire*, which was produced at the Pasadena Playhouse and the Wilshire Ebell Theatre. The noted actor, Charlie Chaplin, aided Dunne in producing the play off-Broadway in Blackfriars Theatre, and in Chicago, where it was reviewed by Langston Hughes. Dunne challenged the racial prejudice of his time, but his activism for social justice led to his dismissal from Loyola's faculty and his transfer out of the archdiocese of Los Angeles (Dunne, 1945, 1946, 1950, 1990; Spickard, 2000). The persistent influence of the exiled Dunne, and of others in a short-lived Catholic Interracial Council on campus, roused the ire of the new archbishop of Los Angeles, James Francis McIntyre. The prelate resolutely maintained that Los Angeles had no race problem, save what was incited by outside agitators (Tighe, Jr., personal interview, October 17, 1992). The Council quickly disbanded.

Shortly after Dunne's transfer, a new president assumed leadership at Loyola, the man most responsible for building a modern university out of a small college. Reverend Charles S. Casassa, S.J., possessed no previous presidential experience when, at age 39, he began his 20 year tenure. The first president of the school with an earned doctorate (in philosophy), Casassa raised the academic standing of the school and proved to be an adept fundraiser. While erecting nine buildings on the Westchester campus, he also secured a new site for the Law School on West Ninth Street (now James Wood Boulevard). Casassa also fostered an ecumenical spirit, particularly with the Jewish community, where he stood almost alone among Los Angeles' Catholic leaders.

Three events highlight Casassa's record and demonstrate his philosophy of Catholic education and human rights. The first example concerns Loyola's football program, which dated back to Father Sullivan's tenure. The Loyola Lions in 1950 were ranked 19th nationally in football, and inspired dreams of the school's first invitation to a post-season bowl. Alumni enthusiasm ran high until Casassa chose to forfeit a game in late September 1950 against Texas Western University, now known as the University of Texas-El Paso. The Regents of the University of Texas then maintained a rule that no African-American could play, either on the teams of their schools or of their opponents. Loyola University was fielding a squad that was all white, except for one African-American player, a starting defensive back named Bill English. When Casassa learned of the Texas regulations, he negotiated with Texas officials, who suggested that if Loyola relented, this rule would not be enforced at the Sun Bowl, to which Loyola would probably be invited. Casassa decided, and the coach,

Jordan Olivar concurred: everyone on the squad played or no one played. Loyola forfeited the game, much to the ire of alumni fans— and to the praise of several fellow Jesuit schools across the nation (*Los Angeles Loyolan*, 1950; Marshall, 1950). (In the last game of the season, an undefeated Loyola fell to the University of Santa Clara, and no bowl bid ever came Loyola's way.)

The second area in which Casassa made a significant contribution to the University was in the establishment of the Human Relations Workshop, which began in 1953 and continued in various forms until the late 1980s. The purpose of this six-week summer institute was to train teachers, police, and public officials in improving community and racial relations within the Los Angeles area. The first director, Reverend Albert S. Foley, S.J., was a professor of sociology at Spring Hill College in Mobile, Alabama. Foley received his doctorate at the University of North Carolina and a post-doctoral fellowship at the Research Center for Group Dynamics at the University of Michigan. Casassa worked in partnership with the local branch of the American Jewish Committee. Together they funded the institute and assembled an Advisory Committee that included distinguished civic leaders like John A. McCone, attorney Martin Gang, and prominent figures such as Irving Stone and Bob Hope (Engh, 2000; *Summary Report*, 1953).

Thirty participants enrolled that first summer (including four members of the Los Angeles Police Department) and attended lectures from a series of guest speakers. Intensive training in inter-group dynamics also included the then new practice of roleplaying. Workshop students also went on a series of field trips to public housing projects, jails, schools, and screenings of a series of films (Foley, 1954; *Summary Report*, 1953). One of the participants, an African-American in the L.A.P.D., later told Foley that he was a disenchanted and disillusioned police officer, but the Workshop dramatically influenced his life. Tom Bradley decided to complete his law degree and to enter politics, and eventually was elected mayor of Los Angeles for five terms. When Bradley received an honorary degree from LMU in 1974, he publicly praised Foley and the Workshop because it had "turned his life around" (Foley, 1985).

Foley returned annually to conduct the successful and well-received Workshop until 1957 when Archbishop McIntyre, of Los Angeles, claimed to detect the actions of Communists and fellow trav-

elers at Loyola. McIntyre forbade Foley to return or to speak anywhere in the archdiocese of Los Angeles. When Foley protested by letter, McIntyre contacted the superior general of the Jesuits, Reverend
John Baptiste Janssens, to demand Foley's apology and obedience.
Foley later recalled that the Workshop had actually been organized, in
part, because of McIntyre's actions and policies. Specifically, one of
the principle aims of the Human Relations Workshop at Loyola
was ". . . to counteract the blatant anti-Semitism that Cardinal
McIntyre was manifesting both in archdiocesan policies and in the
pages of the archdiocesan weekly, the Los Angeles *Tidings*" (Foley,
1954, p. 314–316).

The third achievement for which Casassa warrants our consideration developed out of a further encounter with the Archbishop of
Los Angeles during the course of Vatican II. After the first session of
the council had recessed in January of 1963, the University invited
Reverend Hans Kung, a *peritus* at the council and professor of theology at the University of Tubingen, to speak on campus during a
nationwide lecture tour. Casassa approached McIntyre for the requi-
site permission, which was refused, on the grounds that students were
insufficiently prepared for the level of theological discourse expected
from Kung. Casassa persisted until McIntyre relented to the extent
that the faculty was permitted to hear Kung. Over 300 people attended Kung's presentation on April 3, 1963, in St. Robert's Auditorium,
and at the open windows students thronged outside to hear (Krebs,
1964; Weber, 1997).

During the Casassa years, Reverend Clint Albertson, S.J.
(English), Professor Anthony Turhollow (History), and Father Alex
Humphreys, S.J. (Sociology) founded the Honors Program in 1958.
This trio assured Casassa that the program would not cost the school
anything to operate and would enhance the University's academic
standing. Limited to 12 new students each year, the first 40 graduates
of the program distinguished themselves upon graduating when each
man received honors, awards, or fellowships (Albertson, personal
interview, 2000). From this group came the University's first Rhodes
Scholar, Brian Fay (whom Mike Rose misidentified as Brian Kelly),
who later graduated with two degrees from Oxford University and
then proceeded to teach philosophy at Wesleyan University (Rose,
1989).

In the mid-1960s, a group of University Regents approached Father Casassa with another proposal and urged him to start a program in Communication Studies. Men, such as Edward Foley, believed that the University should introduce Catholic philosophy and values into the media of Hollywood. Casassa delegated this task to the dean of the College of Arts and Sciences, Reverend Terrance L. Mahan, S.J., who, in 1962, supervised the creation of an interdisciplinary program using existing faculty. Focusing on "writing for press, radio, film, and television," the popularity of these studies led to undergraduate and graduate degree programs, and to the College of Communication and Fine Arts (*Loyola Marymount of Los Angeles Brochure*, n.d.). In 1964, Casassa requested permission from Cardinal McIntyre for Loyola to admit women to the undergraduate program of the University. After consulting the presidents of the Catholic women's colleges in the city, McIntyre refused, citing the harm that would come to these schools if Loyola changed its admissions policy.

So matters rested at Loyola, while at Marymount College dramatic change was taking place. Because of continued growth, the Sisters decided to build a separate campus for the college. Learning that the California State University system would establish a South Bay branch, the longtime president, Mother Gertrude Cain, R.S.H.M., located the new campus on 45 acres on the Palos Verdes Peninsula (Kearney, 1965). Her successor, Mother Sacre Couer Smith, R.S.H.M., began construction, but died suddenly in 1964. Mother M. Raymunde McKay, R.S.H.M., departed the presidency at Marymount Manhattan College to meet the emergency and to assume the leadership in Palos Verdes (Engh, 2000).

McKay assessed the situation she found and spoke forthrightly about the significant challenges confronting the school. She believed that the curriculum needed "a stimulant," so she introduced a yearlong, tri-term program, with a six-week winter term. First-year students immersed themselves in foreign language, conversation, civilization, and literature; sophomores studied the fine arts. Juniors and seniors conducted independent studies, either on or off campus. While revamping the course of studies, McKay learned that the administrators of the California State University system had decided to build their new branch at Dominguez Hills (McKay, personal interview, 1996). This decision left Marymount College isolated, both socially and academically, which gravely threatened future enrollment.

Further, the accelerating national trend towards coeducational collegiate education also worried leaders of the all-women's college.

McKay took two imaginative steps to confront these challenges. She began by approaching Casassa about a partnership or affiliation of Marymount and Loyola. Hearing from Casassa of McIntyre's
opposition to coeducation, McKay skillfully proposed to McIntyre
that Loyola and Marymount initiate "co-instruction" at the Westchester campus. McIntyre readily agreed, much to the astonishment of
Casassa (McKay, personal interview, 1996). Marymount College relocated to the Loyola campus, and the schools began sharing one another's facilities and faculties in the fall of 1968. Marymount brought to the Jesuit campus a strong tradition in the arts (both
studio arts and art history), as well as creative academic programs in
ethnic studies, international education, a reentry course of study for
nontraditional students to complete their degrees, and a second community of women religious (Loonam, personal interview 1995).

McKay's second bold initiative was to enlist the larger community of the Sisters of St. Joseph of Orange as partners in supporting
Marymount College. Possessing a collegiate program in the city of
Orange for the training of their members, the Sisters of St. Joseph
counted a respectable number of trained administrators and faculty
members holding doctorates (Geagley, 1986). The sudden drop in
Sisters' vocations in the mid-1960s left the Orange program over-
staffed, so McKay proposed that the two religious communities join as
partners to sponsor Marymount College. When Marymount moved to
Loyola, both women's religious communities arrived. Women's enrollment at Marymount began to rise, and a broader array of courses
and instructors were available to both male and female students. By
1969, the Marymount College *Faculty Handbook* described the
school's changed vision under McKay's leadership:

> Marymount's philosophy of education is based on the
> premise that the role of woman in society today is different
> from that of man and indeed from what it was for her even
> ten years ago. To take her place in society today a woman
> must have an inquiring and disciplined mind capable of
> pursuing the truth, an intellectual openness that is sensitive
> to diversity and unity, an intimacy with tradition which is
> understood as continuity and culture. Ideally, she should
> have developed a deep appreciation of the beautiful so that

every event and person speaks to her of ultimate Beauty.
(*Marymount College Faculty Handbook*, 1969)

After five years of duplicating administrations, boards, and certain departments, the two schools agreed to merge. In 1973, Reverend Donald P. Merrifield, S.J., Casassa's successor, was named first president of Loyola Marymount University, while McKay assumed the newly created post of Provost. Numerous difficulties challenged the University in the next 20 years, not the least of which were issues concerning gender equity and the racial diversification of the student body and the faculty. Responding to changes in church and in society, Merrifield initiated programs to promote social justice both on and off campus (Engh, 1989). He fostered efforts to recruit greater numbers of minority students, as did his successors, James Loughran, S.J. (1984–1991), Thomas P. O'Malley, S.J. (1991–1999), and Robert Lawton, S.J. (1999-present). Merrifield also worked with Casassa in the area of ecumenism, particularly in continued contacts with the Jewish community of Los Angeles, for which he received an honorary doctorate from Hebrew Union College-Jewish Institute of Religion in 1986 (Vadakin & Wolf, 1986).

Also during his tenure as president, Merrifield oversaw important construction on the Westchester campus to accommodate an expanding curriculum and a growing residential student population. Worthy of note is the Wil and Mary Jane Von der Ahe Communication Arts building which opened in 1971 to house the expanding offerings in film and television production. In 1984, the University acquired 27 acres of land from the Summa Corporation, later named the Leavey Campus. Merrifield also approved the hiring of the then-rising architect, Frank O. Gehry, to design new facilities for the Loyola Law School. By 1993, Gehry's genius produced five striking buildings and a parking structure for a campus that the Whitney Library of Design listed in its *20ᵗʰ Century American Architecture: A Traveler's Guide to 220 Key Buildings* (LeBlanc, 1996).

Under James Loughran, S.J., significant changes affected the faculty and the entire school. Loughran worked to reduce the faculty teaching load from eight courses per year to six (three both semesters). He envisioned this as a means to enable faculty to engage in more serious scholarly and creative work in their respective disciplines. Further, Loughran's administration convoked a blue-ribbon Commission on the Future of Loyola Marymount University, which completed its work in 1989 under the leadership of Robert F. Erburu, chief executive officer of the Times-Mirror Corporation, and Roland Seilder, Jr., chair of the LMU Board of Trustees (*Future of Loyola Marymount University Commission Report*, 1989).

For two years, 239 civic leaders on the Commission reviewed operations of all aspects of the University and listened to its constituencies. They issued a 34 page assessment that both affirmed many University programs and challenged the school to go further. The report urged the school to give priority to attracting Latinos and African-Americans (particularly males). It stated that LMU should limit enrollment increases in certain colleges in order ". . . to attract more women and ethnic minorities to fields in which they are underrepresented," (such as science and engineering) (*Future of Loyola Marymount University Commission Report*, 1989, p.22). This blueprint for the direction of the University led to a new Mission and Goals statement, as well as to a revision of the core curriculum, with the addition of two requirements: a second fine arts course, and an American Cultures class to bring the benefits of racial and ethnic diversity into the curriculum (Jabbra, 1990, 1991; *Loyola Marymount University Mission & Goals*, 1990). Significantly, all this occurred prior to the 1992 civil unrest in Los Angeles.

During Loughran's administration, the Religious of the Sacred Heart of Mary established the Marymount Institute for Faith, Culture and the Arts. In 1989, the Sisters recommitted themselves to fostering the creative interaction between faith and the arts by endowing this Center. The Center sponsored lectures, creative works, and a faculty grant program for interdisciplinary course development on specified topics. Ten years later, the Institute announced the creation of the Marymount Chair of Interdisciplinary Studies to enable an LMU faculty member to ". . . create, coordinate, and teach an interdisciplinary course bringing together faith, the riches of culture, humanities and the arts" (*Marymount Institute for Faith, Culture and the Arts Flyer*, 1999). In the spring semester of 2000, the Institute awarded the first two-year chair to Theresia de Vroom, Ph.D., of the English department.

Thomas P. O'Malley, S.J., built on the foundations of his predecessors, so that diversification within the student body and faculty reached unprecedented numbers, both for the University and among all Jesuit colleges and universities in the United States (*Loyola*

Marymount University Statistical Handbook, 2000). The Law School student body grew to be the second-most diverse student population in the United States, while in the state of California it was the first ABA-accredited law school to establish an uncompensated public service requirement (*Loyola Law School Fact Sheet*, 1998). Through the Irvine Grant program, the James Irvine Foundation also enabled the University to increase the hiring of minority faculty members. These and other efforts earned the University the Theodore M. Hesburgh Award for 1998 from the Teachers' Insurance and Annuity Association-College Retirement Equities Fund (TIAA-CREF) for ". . . faculty development to enhance undergraduate teaching and learning" (Medina, 1997).

Further achievements of O'Malley were the establishment of endowed chairs of ethics in each of the colleges of the University, as well as an annual scholarship for an undocumented person. In the summer of 1997, O'Malley saw the LMU Chorus, under the direction of Dr. Mary Breden, achieve new recognition when it was invited to sing at Carnegie Hall. O'Malley initiated and completed a $144 million capital fund drive known as the Campaign for Loyola Marymount, and in 1999 retired to Boston College. After a national search, Reverend Robert Lawton, S.J., of Georgetown University, accepted LMU's invitation to lead the institution and was inaugurated in October, 1999.

Lawton continued plans begun under O'Malley and in January 2000 completed negotiations for the purchase of the one-million-square-foot Raytheon building contiguous to the Leavey Campus of the University. Lawton also began a strategic planning process, enunciated five major goals for the University, and elevated the department of Film and Television to the status of a School. Amidst these significant developments, the University continued to adapt to the changes begun decades earlier when the Roman Catholic Church, under Pope John XXIII, initiated efforts at *aggiornamento*, reform and renewal.

III. Changes in the Roman Catholic Church and in the University since 1965

Both the Society of Jesus and the Religious of the Sacred Heart of Mary received inspiration and mandates to change from meetings of the hierarchy of the Roman Catholic Church: the Second

Vatican Council (1962–1965), and the Second Synod of Bishops (1971). These two international gatherings issued important documents that affected the renewal and direction of all religious orders. In several of their statements, the bishops of Vatican II enunciated their understanding of the nature of the Church and its mission in the modern world. They noted that members of the laity have particular and important roles to play and significant talents to offer the Church, free of clerical paternalism (Abbott & Gallagher, 1966). The Council began the process to end the custodial attitude towards the laity and to encourage their "empowerment." The Fathers of the Council also urged religious communities to return to the original inspiration or "charism" of their founders in order to reinvigorate their works and to renew their orders.

In 1971, the Synod of Bishops produced one of the turning-point documents in the history of the modern Catholic Church. Deeply concerned about the growing poverty in the world and the widening gap between the haves and the have-nots, they were alarmed that the Church did not address itself directly to the structural and systemic inequities in national and international economies. The bishops wrote: "Action on behalf of justice and participation in the transformation of the world fully appear to us as a constitutive dimension of preaching the Gospel . . ." (O'Brien, 1971; O'Brien & Shannon, 1992). Every religious order in the Catholic world met and discussed the implications of these new directives from Rome and the bishops, and repeatedly returned to these texts for inspiration and guidance.

The Jesuits' response came in an assembly known as a General Congregation, with delegates from every Jesuit province and region in the world. Meeting in Rome in 1974–1975, they issued a series of statements, one of which, Decree Four, *The Service of Faith and the Promotion of Justice*, committed the Jesuits to a "preferential option for the poor." They redirected the Order when they concluded that: "The mission of the Society of Jesus today is the service of faith, of which the promotion of justice is an absolute requirement. . . . Injustice is not only personal but institutionalized: built into economic, social, and political structures that dominate the life of nations and the international community . . ."(*Documents of the 31st and 32nd General Congregation*, 1977, pp. 411–412, 428).

Similar commitments can also be found in the revised constitutions of the Religious of the Sacred Heart of Mary, approved in

1983. "Faithful to our heritage, attentive to the signs of the times and the call of the Church, we are committed to the service of evangelical justice, wherever we are and whatever our ministry" (*Constitutions of the Institute of the Religious of the Sacred Heart of Mary Immaculate Virgin*, 1983). The implications of "the service of faith and the promotion of justice" challenged educators around the world, and the principle has set deep roots in the psyche of the Marymount Sisters and the Jesuits (Tripole, 1999).

For Catholic higher education, the most dramatic example of the application of the summons to faith and justice took place at the Jesuits' University of Central America in El Salvador, when six of the priests and two lay workers were murdered in November, 1989. The school's rector (president), Ignacio Ellacuria, S.J., had proclaimed that a Jesuit university must work to ". . . provide science for those who have no science; to provide skills for the unskilled; to be a voice for those who have no voice; to give intellectual support for those who do not possess the academic qualifications to promote and legitimate their rights" (Whitfield, personal interview, 1994). Commitment to these goals costs the Jesuits and their workers their lives.

Coinciding with these social justice developments, religious orders in the United States welcomed members of the laity to the administration of the colleges and universities that priests, brothers, and nuns had founded. The Jesuits and Religious of the Sacred Heart of Mary recruited and established civil boards of trustees to which they entrusted the ownership and operation of these schools (Fitzgerald, 1984). This movement swept the United States in the late 1960s and early 1970s for a variety of reasons, both ecclesial and financial. Thus, neither the Jesuits nor the Sisters continued to own the University. Vatican authorities have struggled to understand these American developments and began insisting that the Catholic colleges and universities in the United States take appropriate steps to remain truly Catholic.

In his 1990 document, *Ex Corde Ecclesiae*, Pope John Paul II spelled out the principles of the relationship between the Roman Catholic Church and Catholic universities throughout the world. He also asked the bishops of each nation to draft norms for the application of these ideals to their respective countries. The American traditions of academic freedom and of separation of church and state proved difficult to synthesize with the papal mandate. With 235 universities and colleges in this country, American Catholics have the largest number of such institutions of any nation in the world. After a decade of discussions and drafts, the Vatican accepted the bishops' statement of guidelines in November 1999 (U.S. Catholic Bishops Conference, 2000). These norms went into effect in May, 2001. College presidents are presently educating the members of their boards of trustees about the requirements that the norms stipulate. The first five years of implementation are slated to be a period of dialogue and review between bishops and the leaders of Catholic higher education (Robert & Turner, 2000; U.S. Catholic Bishops Conference, 2000).

The decade of discussions about *Ex Corde Ecclesiae* focused widespread attention on defining the distinctive characteristics of American Catholic higher education. Certain authors maintained that Catholic schools had lost all distinguishing qualities in their pursuit of secular academic excellence (Burtchaell, 1998). Others noted a renewal of concern and widespread creative responses to promoting collegiate experiences that were both intellectually rigorous and deeply rooted in the Catholic tradition (Modras, 1995). It became apparent that, more than ever, Catholic institutions required an informed laity to guide their schools. Their material success and the social acceptance of American Catholics have shifted the challenges that Catholics and their universities face. Leaders today must be grounded in the living traditions of their respective institutions, while exercising creative leadership in order to integrate religious and ethical values throughout the curriculum, in student life, among the boards of trustees, and in the ethos of the institution.

Elsewhere in the world, in the year 2000, the Marymount Sisters were present in 14 countries and offered primary, secondary, and collegiate education in 34 institutions, while individual Sisters worked in dozens of other schools operated by diocese or other religious congregations (Milligan, personal interview, 2000). Looking beyond national boundaries, their goal remained to promote the life and dignity of all. The most recent statistics for Jesuit institutions date from 1998 and listed 177 colleges, universities, graduate schools, and seminaries operated by the Society of Jesus. (Twenty-eight of these colleges and universities are in the United States.) Besides work in higher education, the Jesuits also seek "the service of faith and the promotion of justice" through the 1,434 primary, middle, secondary, and special schools they operate worldwide (*Statistical Report on Education in the Society [of Jesus]*, 1998).

Conclusion

These developments bring us to the present, where a historian such as myself treads cautiously while looking to the past and recalling those whose successes and failures created this University. The history of this school includes the significant shift in the Catholic approach to faith from a custodial model to one of empowerment. Also, the concern in the last three decades for "the service of faith and the promotion of justice" coincides with the development of new institutional ways to incarnate the Catholic nature of Loyola Marymount University. Finally, this history rests on the imagination and accomplishments of people such George Dunne, Charles Casassa, and Raymunde McKay. Committed to the moral and intellectual traditions of the Catholic Church, they used these beliefs to meet creatively the evolving social and educational challenges of their times. Current reflection on the nature of the University draws us deeper in this history and closer to our creative tradition. As current faculty, we are the ones who now embody the intellectual and imaginative life of the Catholic university. Like the professors who educated a young Mike Rose, we continue to invite students to explore the world of the mind and we strive to inspire in them a passion to learn. In our classrooms we launch those quests that begin in solitary musings, continue in dorm-room discussions, and persist in students' lives long after they depart the University. We choose what issues to probe, which resources to utilize, what interpretations to explore.

Though we possess the legacy of the Catholic imagination, we may not know how best to use this rich, varied, and dynamic asset for intellectual exploration. We can enrich ourselves by examining how scholars have for, centuries, perceived by means of this Catholic tradition the ways that the transcendent illumines our world and how the human touches the divine. By such learning and through continued excellent teaching, we reincarnate the intellectual heritage that distinguishes the Catholic university. Our recourse to this Catholic way of imagining enhances our efforts to offer that "best sort of liberal education" so cherished by our alumni and so needed in the Church and society. Knowing our heritage, we stand closer to Loyola, Gailhac,

Cure-Pelissier, Aquinas, Augustine, and, ultimately, to the Word first spoken by the Divine.

REFERENCES

Abbott, W., S.J., & Gallagher, J. (1966). *Pastoral Constitution on the Church in the Modern World. The Documents of Vatican II.* New York, NY: Guild Press.

Bailey, B., R.S.H.M., & McMahaon, B., R.S.H.M., (Eds.). (1999). *Like a River: Religious of the Sacred Heart of Mary—150 Years (n.p.).* [On-line]. Available: Religious Heart of Mary Website www.rshm.org.

Bernardin, J. (1996, May 4). "What makes a hospital Catholic— A response." *America, 174* (45), 9-11.

Bradshaw, J. (1972, August 6). "The club game: Any number can't play." *Los Angeles Times Magazine,* 7-8.

Bulletin (1947-1948). Los Angeles, CA: Loyola University.

Bulletin (1948). Los Angeles, CA: Loyola University.

Burtchaell, J. T. (1998). *The Dying of the Light: The Disengagement of Colleges and Universities from their Christian Churches.* Grand Rapids, MI: Eerdmans.

Cantwell, J. J. (1922, May 27). Letter, to Reverend Mother Mary Joseph Butler Religious of Sacred Heart. Available from the Archives of the Archdiocese of Los Angeles, California.

Codina, G., S.J. (2000). "A century of Jesuit education, 1900-2000." In de Vera, J.M., S.J., *Yearbook of the Society of Jesus, 2000.* Rome: General Curia of the Society of Jesus, 2000.

Commission Members Notebook (1988). Los Angeles, CA: Loyola Marymount University.

Connell, K., R.S.H.M. (1993). "A journey in faith and time: history of the Religious of the Sacred Heart of Mary, 2: The growth of the institute: The foundations during Mother St. Croix Vidal's leadership, 1869–1878." *Religious Sacred Heart of Mary* (pp. 121–132, 199–217). Rome: *Religious of the Sacred Heart of Mary.*

Constitutions of the Institute of the Religious of the Sacred Heart of Mary Immaculate Virgin (1983). Rome: *Religious of the Sacred Heart of Mary.*

Constitutions of the Society of Jesus and Their Complementary norms (1996). St. Louis, MO: Institute of Jesuit Sources.

Do Campo Sampaio, R., R.S.H.M. (1990). "A journey in faith and time: History of the Religious of the Sacred Heart of Mary, 1: The birth of the Institute: Its development during Mother St. Jean's lifetime." *Religious Sacred Heart of Mary* (pp. 9–170) Rome: *Religious of the Sacred Heart of Mary.*

Documents of the 31st and 32nd General Congregations of the Society of Jesus (1977). St. Louis, MO: Institute of Jesus Sources.

Documents of the 34th General Congregation of the Society of Jesus (1995). St. Louis, MO: Institute of Jesuit Sources.

Dolan, J. P. (1985). *The American Catholic Experience: A History from Colonial Times to the Present.* Garden City, NJ: Doubleday and Company.

Dunne, G. H., S.J. (1945, September 21). "The sin of segregation." *Commonwealth, 21,* 542–645.

Dunne, G. H., S.J. (1946, March 1). "The short case." *Commonwealth, 43,* 494–497.

Dunne, G. H., S.J. (1950, October 6). "And who is my neighbor?" *Commonwealth, 44,* 134–138.

Dunne, G. H., S.J. (1990). *King's Pawn.* Chicago, IL: Loyola University Press.

Ellacuria, I., S.J. (1994). "The task of a Christian university." In T. Whitfield, *Paying the price: Ignacio Ellacuria and the murdered Jesuits of El Salvador.* Philadelphia, PA: Temple University Press.

Engh, M. E., S.J. (1989, January). "Charity knows neither race nor creed." *Western States Jewish History, 21*, 154–165.

Engh, M. E., S.J. (2000). "Just ones past and present at Loyola Marymount University." In M.K. McCullough (Ed.), *The Just One Justices: The Role of Justice at the Heart of Catholic Higher Education* (pp. 21–36). Scranton, PA: University of Scranton Press.

First Annual Catalogue of Los Angeles College (1911–1912). Los Angeles, CA: Los Angeles College.

Fitzgerald, P . A., S.J. (1984). *The Governance of Jesuit Colleges in the United States, 1920–1970*. Notre Dame, IN: University of Notre Dame Press.

Foley, A. S., S.J. (1954, November). "The Workshop Way." *Interracial Review*.

Foley, A. S., S.J. (1985). Untitled manuscript. Albert S. Foley, S.J., Collection, Archives of the New Orleans Province of the Society of Jesus. New Orleans, Louisiana.

Future of Loyola Marymount University Commission Report (1989). Los Angeles, CA: Loyola Marymount University.

Ganss, G.E., S.J. (1992). *The Spiritual Exercises of Saint Ignatius* (trans.). Chicago, IL: Loyola University Press.

Geagley, B. (1986). *A Compassionate Presence: In celebration of the 75th Year in California, The Story of the Sisters of St. Joseph of Orange*. Orange, CA: Sisters of St. Joseph of Orange.

Gleason, P. (1987). *Keeping the Faith: American Catholicism Past and Present*. Notre Dame, IN: University of Notre Dame Press.

Gleason, P. (1995). *Contending with Modernity: Catholic Higher Education in the Twentieth Century*. New York, NY: Oxford University Press.

Gussenhoven, F., R.S.H.M. (1985, March 15). *The Meaning of Marymount at LMU*. Los Angeles, CA. Loyola Marymount University.

Jabbra, J.G. (1990, February). *"Report of the Select Committee on Minorities."* Los Angeles, CA: Loyola Marymount University, Academic Vice President.

Jabbra, J. G. (1991, February 11). *Memorandum.* Paper in possession of author.

Jesuit Educational Statistics (1993). Rome, Italy: Curia of the Society of Jesus. [On-line]. Available: www.jesuit.org/resources/ highered.

John Paul II (1990). *Ex Corde Ecclesiae* (Vatican, trans.). Boston, MA: Pauline Books.

Kearney, S. I., R.S.H.M. (1965). *Foundations of Faith.* Tarrytown, NY: Privately printed.

Krebs, A. V. (1964, July 10). "A Church of silence." *Commonwealth, 80,* 472.

LeBlanc, S. (1996). *20th Century American Architecture: A Traveler's Guide to 220 Key Buildings* (2nd ed.). New York, NY: Whitney Library of Design.

Los Angeles Loyolan (1950, October 3). p. 3.

Loyola Law School Fact Sheet (1998). Los Angeles, CA: Loyola Law School.

Loyola Marymount of Los Angeles—Communication Arts Program Brochure. Los Angeles, CA: Loyola Marymount University.

Loyola Marymount University: Mission, Goals and Objectives (1990, November). Los Angeles, CA: Loyola Marymount University.

Loyola Marymount University Statistical Handbook (2000). Los Angeles, CA: Loyola Marymount University.

Loyola University of Los Angeles (1947). *Bulletin 1947–1948.* Los Angeles, CA: Loyola University.

Lucas, T. M., S.J. (2000). "Location, location, location." *Conversations in Jesuit Higher Education,* 17.

Marsden, G. M. (1994). *The Soul of the American University*. New York, NY: Oxford University Press.

Marymount College Faculty Handbook (1969). Los Angeles, CA: Marymount College.

Marymount Institute for Faith, Culture, and the Arts Flyer (1999). Los Angeles, CA: Loyola Marymount University.

Marymount School Catalogue (1936). Los Angeles, CA: Marymount School.

McDonough, P. (1992). *Men Astutely Trained: A History of the Jesuits in the American Century*. New York, NY: Free Press.

McKevitt, G., S.J. (1991, October). "Jesuit Higher Education in the United States." *MidAmerica*.

Medina, H. (1997). *Growing Together as a Multicultural Community: A Response to the Events in Los Angeles in Spring 1992*. From the application of the Hesburgh Award.

Modras, R. (1995, February 4). "The spiritual humanism of the Jesuits." *America, 172*, (3), 10–18.

Morris, C.R. (1997). *American Catholic: The saints and Sinners Who Built America's Most Powerful Church*. New York, NY: Random House.

O'Brien, D.J. (1971). "The American priest and social action." In J.T. Ellis (Ed.), *The Catholic Priest in the United States: Historical Investigations*. Collegeville, MN: St. John's University Press.

O'Brien, D. J., & Shannon, T. A., (Eds.) (1992). *Catholic Social Thought: The Documentary Heritage*. "Justice in the world." Second General Assembly of the Synod of Bishops. Maryknoll, NY: Orbis.

O'Malley, J.W. (1993). *The First Jesuits*. Cambridge, MA: Harvard University Press.

O'Malley, J.W. (1999). "Introduction in Atteberry & Russell" (Eds.). *Ratio Studiorum, 10*.

Ravitch, D. (1974). *The Great School Wars: New York City, 1805-1973*. New York, NY: Basic Books.

Report of the Commission of the Future of Loyola Marymount University (1988–1989). Los Angeles, CA:Loyola Marymount University.

Robert, J. H., & Turner, J. (2000). *The Sacred and the Secular University*. Princeton, PA: Princeton University Press.

Rose, M. (1989). *Lives on the Boundary: The Struggles and Achievements of America's Underprepared*. New York, NY: Free Press.

Spickard, P. R. (2000, Fall). "Fire in the night: A 1945 Southern California hate crime and historical memory." *Southern California Quarterly*, 291–304.

Stammer, L. B. (1996, November 14). "Catholic bishops ok new academic freedom rules." *Los Angeles Times*, pp. A1, A32.

Statistical Handbook, Loyola Marymount University, 1999–2000 (1999). p. 3. Los Angeles, CA: Office of Institutional Research, Loyola Marymount University.

Statistical Report on Education in the Society [of Jesus] (1998). St. Louis, MO: Institute of Jesuit Sources.

Summary Report: Human Relations Workshop, Loyola University (1953, April). In [1-3]; Box 16D/1. Department of University Archives and Special Collections, Charles Von der Ahe Library, Loyola Marymount University, Los Angeles, CA.

Education S. J. (1998, December). Statistical report on education in the society [of Jesus]. p. 5.

"The Jews and the Jonathon Club" (1905, April 22). *The Graphic*, 22, 9.

The Marymount Institute for Faith, Culture and the Arts Announce the Marymount Chair of Interdisciplinary Studies (1999, November 1). Flyer.

Tripole, M. R., S.J. (Ed.). (1999). *Promise Renewed: Jesuit Higher Education for a New Millenium.* Chicago, IL: Loyola Press.

U.S. Catholic Bishops Conference (2000, June 15). "*Ex Corde Ecclesiae*": An application to the United States," Washington D.C. *Origins, 20,* (5).

Vadakin, R. M. Msgr., & Wolf, A., Rabbi. (1986). "The Los Angeles story." In E.J. Fisher, J. Rudin, & M.H. Tanenbaum, (Eds.), *Twenty Years of Jewish-Catholic Relations* (p. 157). New York, NY: Paulist Press.

Vorspan, M., & Gartner, L. (1970). *History of the Jews of Los Angeles.* San Marino, CA: Huntington Library.

Weber, F. J. (1970). "What ever happened to St. Vincent's College?" *Pacific Historian, 14.*

Weber, F. J. (1997). *His Eminence of Los Angeles: James Francis Cardinal McIntyre, II.* Mission Hills, CA: St. Francis Historical Society.

On Being Catholic and American

Robert N. Bellah

How is it that a Protestant, of Scotch-Irish descent, who is undoubtedly related, if you go back far enough, to those dreadful people who go around marching in Northern Ireland every summer, should write on the subject "On Being Catholic and American"? That very fact may be an indication of where we are in this matter. If there had been no Vatican II there would probably not have been a Graduate Theological Union (GTU) in Berkeley, at least not one that included both Catholic and Protestant schools, and I would not have spent over 30 years working closely with Catholic professors and students as an Adjunct Professor at the GTU. There is also the fact that three of my four coauthors of *Habits of the Heart*— and *The Good Society*, were raised Catholic. Not only that, but each in his own way has had a serious experience of the religious life, most notably Richard Madsen, who was a Maryknoll father for years and is still a close advisor to the Maryknoll order. So I have been pretty well socialized into what Andrew Greeley (2000) calls "the Catholic imagination" over the years.

And finally, there is the fact that, though I was raised a Presbyterian, my own intellectual and spiritual development has led me to the Episcopal Church, which, while not Catholic, is not exactly Protestant either. Hans Kung (1995), in his book *Christianity: Essence, History, and Future,* after discussing the Anglican Church as a kind of middle way between Catholicism and the Reformation, says that perhaps ". . . the whole of the Catholic church could have looked like this" (p. 596) if there had been a compromise between Luther and Rome in the 16th century; that is, an international communion (he points out that among Protestants only the Anglicans have a real worldwide communion), but considerably decentralized and allowing for a great deal of diversity at the national level, within the context of a strong sacramentalism. That may seem a horrifying idea, if it is thinkable at all, but for me it has a certain charm.

While there is no golden age that we can look back to with nostalgia, and it is also true that throughout the history of the church there have been potential or actual conflicts, heresies, and schisms, it is the case that up until the 16th century Catholicism was largely synonymous with Western culture, whereas since that time the Church, though remaining a significant cultural force, has had to deal with challenges, alternatives, and rivals. It might be well to sketch briefly the several waves of modernity in which these alternatives have been expressed.

There was first of all the Protestant Reformation itself, which I, following Weber, see as the single most important moment leading to modernity. The great project of modernity was the leap into freedom. The first step was the claim to spiritual freedom: that individuals can relate directly to God without any mediation. The Reformers saw many Catholic beliefs and practices as forms of magical mediation, and thus attacked the doctrine of transubstantiation, the veneration of saints, and other traditional practices that they deemed magical. In their fear of idolatry they, in effect, pushed God out of the world into radical transcendence. With the doctrine of predestination John Calvin (or if not Calvin, as some scholars now believe, then some of his followers) describes a God who preordains everything that occurs before the beginning of time. It was natural for some philosophers and scientists to move from predestination to a deterministic physical universe without a personal God at all: "I have no need of that hypothesis," as one of them said. So Calvin's powerful doctrine of divine transcendence paradoxically opened the door to atheistic naturalism.

To the extent that the Reformation led to a renewed emphasis on the enfranchisement of the laity, the priesthood of all believers, it was a fulfillment of Christian teachings. And the idea of the priesthood of all believers did help subjects to become citizens when changes in church polity stimulated changes in national polity. But the suspicion of any form of mediation led to a weakening of the very idea of the church itself.

The Enlightenment leapt further into freedom, imagining that we could live by disembodied reason alone. But the next turn in the process of emancipation was the disembedding of the economy from traditional constraints, and the consequent depletion of all those institutions that formerly protected the lifeworld. In the capitalist world the individual was left more alone than ever and vulnerable to the great ideological movements that swept the world in the 20th century, movements that falsely promised security in an increasingly insecure world. At least in the United States a dynamic, open and affluent society was able, for a long time, to slow the corrosive effects of modernization.

But we have now entered a third wave of modernity, characterized by post-modernity at the level of high culture and the collapse of preexisting solidarities throughout the social system, leading to the emergence of the loose connections and the porous institutions that Robert Wuthnow, Robert Putnam, and others have described. Our rather fragile affluence at the moment papers over the deep tears in our social fabric, but any serious challenge would reveal how incoherent our society has become. It is in this context that I want to consider what the Catholic tradition in America has to say to its own adherents and to the larger society.

Here I would affirm Charles Taylor's position in his address "A Catholic Modernity?" namely, that neither a Catholic modernism that jettisons major aspects of the tradition in order to appear contemporary, nor a Catholic integralism that imagines a total rejection of the modern world is a viable alternative. Only by appreciating the genuine achievements of modernity, Taylor argues, will we be in a position to criticize adequately its weaknesses and failings. Only in a genuine dialogue with modernity can Catholics and other believers hope to alter its course. As Taylor writes:

> The view I'd like to defend, if I can put it in a nutshell, is that in modern, secularist culture there are mingled together both authentic developments of the gospel, of an incarnational mode of life, and also a closing off to God that negates the gospel. The notion is that modern culture, in breaking with the structures and beliefs of Christendom, also carries certain facets of Christian life further than they ever were taken or could have been taken within Christendom. In relation to the earlier forms of Christian culture, we have to face the humbling realization that the breakout was a necessary condition of the development. (Taylor, 1999, p. 16)

As examples of the achievements of modernity Taylor cites universal human rights and the appreciation of ordinary life. But, Taylor warns, a radically secularist view which denies that rights and life come from anything beyond rights and life endangers the very achievements of modernity and cries out for a deeper understanding of the human condition in relation to God.

There is much more to be said about modernity and its pitfalls, and much more about the problems of contemporary American society. However, I want to focus on intellectual life and its embodiment in American universities. It is common for people in my position to discuss the positivism, scientism, naturalism, and reductionism which have become so central in our intellectual life and in the academy. Much as I see those as critically important issues, I think we need to go back further, especially in the American case, to the heritage of the Reformation which lies behind, and not very far behind, the Enlightenment and its subsequent developments, and which has deeply influenced the American university.

I want to make the argument, with the help of David Tracy (1981), that the Christian theological tradition has included both analogy and dialectic, and that they are mutually corrective. Oversimplifying Tracy's complex argument, the analogical imagination sees similarities in the relationship between God, self, society, and world, but is tempered by the dialectical imagination with its emphasis on dissimilarities. Tracy's irenic account argues for the primacy of emphasis on the analogical side in Catholic theology and the dialectical side in Protestant theology, but for the fruitful complementarity of both approaches in both theological traditions.

I want to be a little less irenic and argue that the dialectical imagination of Protestantism has often become dangerously one-sided. I have already described the Protestant attacks on practices of mediation: If the differences between God and the world are emphasized so much that the gulf becomes unbridgeable, then the possibility of a Godless world begins to make sense. Much as Tracy (1981) is right in emphasizing the dangers of an analogical imagination untempered by a dialectical moment, I think we can see that in our history it is the Protestant overemphasis on negative dialectics that has had the gravest consequences. One way of putting it would be to say that Protestants have emphasized the element of critical judgment, the great negations of the prophetic tradition, at the expense of the affirmation of Being, the capacity to accept the world as God's creation. The critical dialectical moment, which is certainly there at the heart of the tradition, has become unhinged from the other core elements of the tradition, and the result, for good and for ill, is the drastic progress of modernity.

One result of Protestant one-sidedness is a weakening of the classical doctrine of the Trinity. The three persons of the Trinity begin to be treated separately. What was incipient in H. Richard Niebuhr's (1970) *Radical Monotheism and Western Culture* became explicit in James Gustafson's (1983) *Ethics from a Theocentric Perspective*, which opted for a "low Christology" almost indistinguishable from Unitarianism. The tremendous Protestant emphasis on transcendence has the danger of asserting a transcendence without incarnation, Jesus without Christ. If that is a danger that has been inherent in liberal Protestantism for a long time, there is a parallel danger in Evangelicalism: An exclusive emphasis on Jesus that approaches what Tillich (1957) called Jesusolatry. Accepting Jesus as one's personal Lord and Savior is the whole of it and creeds are seen as unnecessary encumbrances. Pentecostalism is subject to the temptation of a unitarianism of the Spirit.

Another one-sided temptation of Protestantism is the emphasis on the Word, often a Word of judgment, at the expense of the Sacrament. Tillich (1957) expressed this danger as follows:

> The classical combination word and sacrament means, in the first place, the word as well as the sacrament. Next it signifies, the sacrament through the word. And it has often been used, especially in Protestantism, as word without sacrament. (p. 98)

The sacramental life is the key to the analogical imagination, the visible signs of things unseen. To weaken it is to upset an essential balance in the Christian life. Word without Sacrament again runs the danger of transcendence without incarnation.

All the one-sided temptations of Protestantism come to a head in its doctrine of the church, where the suspicion of any mediation between the individual and God tends to empty out the tangible reality of the church as the Body of Christ. For awhile the full implications of this move were attenuated by the development of new intermediate forms of loyalty. It has often been pointed out that the Protestant Reformation paved the way for modern nationalism by breaking the hold of the international church and replacing it with state churches instead. But the American case was extreme in fusing the glory of God with the glory of the nation, in a sense of millennial hopes fulfilled: America as redeemer nation for all the world. This understanding of the nation, in Chesterton's words, "the nation with the soul of a church," lingers today but almost as a shadow of what it once was.

The greater danger in Protestant ecclesiology, one that has been evident from within Protestantism for a long time, is that the church is simply dissolved into its constituent individuals. I recently came across a warning from an American Unitarian leader in the middle of the 19th century, Henry W. Bellows (1859), to his fellow Unitarians, which I found almost paradigmatic of the problem with Protestant ecclesiology. Unitarianism historically is an offshoot of Congregationalism and carries tendencies within Congregationalism and Protestantism generally to a kind of logical conclusion. Bellows named that conclusion individualism. As he put it, writing in 1859, ". . . the sufficiency of the Scriptures turns out to be the self-sufficiency of man, and the right of private judgment an absolute independence of Bible or Church."

> No creed but the Scriptures practically abolishes all Scriptures but those of the human heart; nothing between a man's conscience and his God, vacates the Church; and with the church, the Holy Ghost, whose function is usurped by private reason; the Church lapses into what are called Religious Institutions; these into Congregationalism, and Congregationalism into Individualism—and the logical end is the abandonment of the church as an independent institution . . . and the extinction of worship as a separate interest. (Bellows, 1859, p. 156)

That Bellows's comments were prescient is indicated by a 1988–1989 survey which found that one-third of Americans believe that "people have God within them, so churches aren't really necessary." I suspect even some American Catholics believe that.

To use David Tracy's (1981) shorthand terms, these are the consequences when the dialectical imagination overwhelms the analogical imagination. I think it is obvious that they pave the way for the next step in the history of modernity. A fractured Trinity, the loss of a sense of the sacred within the world as evidenced by the sacraments, a purely verbal and private piety: these open the door to a world without God altogether, a world in which ethical ideals may still be expressed, but those ideals are no longer anchored in any larger under-standing of the whole. They are ideals that from now on depend only on the transient proclivities of the individual heart. At that point we are hovering over the abyss of Nietzschean nihilism, though Americans, for the most part, have been too busy to look down and see it.

I want to turn my attention to the American university, using as my major source George Marsden's (1994) *The Soul of the American University*, whose subtitle says it all: *From Protestant Establishment to Established Nonbelief*, and to offer some suggestions about how we as Christians and as Catholics can cope with our present reality.

Marsden (1994) makes the point that all the great American universities of the 20th century, public as well as private, the schools that set the standards for other universities and in good measure gave the Ph.D's to those who would teach in all universities, came out of Protestantism, more particularly liberal Protestantism, and are unintel-ligible without understanding that religious context and its devolution. He gives a number of examples because each of the great universities has its own story, even though the outcome is depressingly similar.

Harvard, founded in the 17th century as a school for training Congregational ministers, became in the late 19th century, under the leadership of a high-church Unitarian—a designation only intelligible in New England—namely Charles Eliot, (whose personal religion has been called "Unitarianism raised to the *nth* degree" [Marsden, 1994, p. 186],) a national university which combined a commitment to sci-ence and professionalism with a new religion of humanity and high culture. Eliot's "Religion of the Future" held that ". . . knowledge of God . . . comes through the knowledge of the best of the race." It was available for wider consumption in the Harvard Classics, "Dr. Eliot's five-foot book shelf" (Marsden, 1994, p. 193). Harvard to this day is not shy about speaking for the cultural elite, although the link between high culture and the incoherent free elective system in the context of continually differentiating specializations that Eliot also fostered has grown ever more frail.

Marsden (1994) takes the University of Chicago, a much younger school than Harvard, but emerging as a great national univer-sity at about the same time, as a quintessential example of a low-church institution, with its strong Baptist identity, at least at the begin-ning. Marsden notes that since the United States is the only modern nation whose culture was shaped predominantly by low-church Protestantism, it is not surprising that institutions of higher learning would reflect this cultural style:

> So with respect to American universities, their pragmatism, their traditionlessness, their competitiveness, their dependence on the market, their resort to advertising, their emphasis on freedom as free enterprise for professors and individual choice for students, their anti-Catholicism, their scientific spirit, their congeniality to business interests, and their tendency to equate Christianity with democracy and service to the nation, all reflect substantial ties to their low-church past. (Marsden, 1994, p. 239)

What linked populist Chicago with elitist Harvard was the evacuation of any substance that might betray their origin in an organic relationship to a church. The Protestant tendency to allow the nation to take the place of the church (Marsden turns Chesterton around by speaking of a church with the soul of a nation), or dissolving the church into its individual members, was expressed in each school (and in many others) in its own way. Yet while these tendencies were taken for granted in America as simply the inevitable process of secularization in the modern world, Marsden (1994) is surely right to point out that not only were these universities Protestant in origin, in spite of their increasing claim to be nonsectarian, but they were part of a Protestant establishment:

> [T]he Protestant establishment was an establishment. By weakening the distinction between church and nation it had claimed the whole nation as its church. Although its doctrines were thus blended with and often subordinated to the liberal ideals of the republic, they were still doctrines. Moreover, they were doctrines with a distinctly Protestant heritage. (p. 404)

What is peculiar about the Protestant establishment, and what kept it obscure to itself as well as to others, is that it was not an established *church*, for it was just the church which had disappeared. This did not make it any less Protestant and the Protestant heritage remains significant to this day, even though most professors currently teaching at these institutions would be distinctly uncomfortable if that were pointed out to them.

Marsden (1994) is aware that the soul of the university resides not just anywhere in the academic body but in one particular part of it: the faculty. Thus he uses representative faculty members as the most effective way to show how the life of the mind is changing. His examples from Harvard and Chicago as they became national universities at the turn of the 20th century are William James and John Dewey, respectively. James and Dewey represented not only their respective institutions, though they did that, but the emergence of serious American academic culture for the first time. James was an example of Harvard's upper-class, high-church Unitarianism (more Emersonian than Swedenborgian) just as Dewey was an example of Chicago's middle class, low-church orientation, though in his case Methodist rather than Baptist. One might even link the contrast between James's radical humanistic individualism and Dewey's instrumentalism and scientism to the same institutional difference.

Yet in spite of the considerable differences between them, they were part of the general intellectual movement that became known as Pragmatism, and for our purposes most significantly, though they continued to take religion seriously, they left not only the churches of their ancestors but Christianity itself behind. Both found new sources of religious meaning without the embarrassment of traditional religion: for James in individual religious experience, for Dewey in the religion of democracy. Both men grew up in the period before the split between liberal Protestantism and Fundamentalism (Marsden points out that Dwight L. Moody, of revivalist fame, was quite popular with both faculty and students on the Yale campus in the 1890s—that's like imagining Jerry Falwell being popular at Yale today), so that they could not ignore "the religious question." Yet the answers they gave left their successors free to wonder why they need concern themselves with the question at all.

But if James and Dewey represent perhaps the single most critical step in the process with which Marsden's book is concerned, namely the shift from Protestant establishment to established nonbelief, that cannot be the whole story. James and Dewey were extraordinary thinkers, among the most perennially interesting that America has ever produced. Perhaps their creative energy is related to their emancipation from traditional religion just as modern Jewish creativ-

ity is often associated with the generation first experiencing emancipation. Be that as it may, when we criticize some of their ideas as
unfounded, and destructive in their consequences, as I believe we
must, we must also recognize how much we have to learn from them.
For example, Hans Joas, a most interesting German Catholic social
theorist who will be coming to Chicago this fall, gives each of them a
chapter in his impressive book, *The Genesis of Values* (2000). Keeping
in mind Charles Taylor's admonition that we neither uncritically
affirm nor deny modernity, we must acknowledge how much we have
to learn from James and Dewey even as we continue to argue with
them.

One final reflection about the story Marsden tells, that did not
come out of his text but occurred to me as I read it, is the contrast
between the American case, and to some extent Protestant cases generally, and what happened in Catholic countries. In one sense it would
seem that things went much worse for Catholic Christianity in the
transition to modernity than it did for Protestantism. In Catholic countries a militant anticlericalism and secularism led to the expulsion of
Christianity from much of higher education and the explicit establishment of nonbelief in a way we have never experienced in this country.
But in another sense the transition to modernity was much more insid-
ious in Protestant countries. Rather than resisting the process of secularization, liberal Protestantism actually assisted it, to the extent that
most people, whether within or without the universities, never even
knew what was happening. (Those whom Marsden calls "the outsiders" knew, but they seldom had access to the broader public.) In
other words, it is late in the day, when believers have been pushed to
or even beyond the margins of academia, that a book like Marsden's
can appear.

I know the history of Catholic higher education is quite different, but Catholics too have been influenced by the very subtlety of the
transition to secularism, so that it is only when that transition is far
advanced that concerns with Catholic identity come to the forefront;
or maybe such concerns have returned after a post-Vatican II period,
when it was assumed that all was well when Catholic universities
became "normal" American universities. One of the burdens of my
talk is that I want to argue that Catholics who are Americans have
imbibed more Protestantism than they might be aware of, because
American culture and American academic culture in particular, are

Protestant to the bone. Marsden wants Protestants to be aware of their own complex history, but I think it is also incumbent on Catholics to take this dimension of "our" history seriously in order to decide how much of the Protestant ambiance in which we all live to appropriate and how much to resist.

But of course the issue is not one simply of appropriation vs. resistance: Following Taylor's (1999) argument in *A Catholic Modernity?* we can see that it is a continuing engagement with modernity, including, for Americans, the deeply Protestant form of our modernity, that is necessary. It is my belief that this is a Catholic moment in American cultural history and that Protestants and Catholics alike badly need an infusion of the analogical imagination to help us overcome the cultural confusion into which we have fallen.

As to how to realize that possibility, let me use exemplars just as Marsden did. But whereas he used the examples of James and Dewey to help us understand how we got into our present predicament, I want to use the examples of Charles Taylor (1999) and Alasdair MacIntyre (1999) to help understand how we might get out of it, remembering that it is the faculty that is the soul of the university and without the right kind of faculty we are not apt to create the kind of university we want.

I could, and in my first draft did, take the time to show that MacIntyre and Taylor are, each in his own way, figures worthy of comparison with James and Dewy, in scope, the seriousness of thought and the wealth of implications that their work opens up. And I could show that the contemporary two, like the older two, have combined a life of scholarship with one of active political engagement (both have had significant encounters with Marxism, for example), and that both are impressive in their relationship to and influence on their students and colleagues. Both have mastered the technical discourse which has dominated late 20th century philosophy, namely analytic philosophy, but neither has been confined by it, nor by the field of philosophy in its current self understanding: both have strong interests in the social sciences, history, and, unusually for scholars today, in theology. They are thus admirable role models for the kind of faculty members who could make a university with a Catholic identity become a reality today; it must be pointed out that neither of them currently teaches at a Catholic university, though MacIntyre did teach at Notre Dame for a number of years.

But I want to suggest what it is in their thought that is so helpful today, that provides resources for current reflection even for those of us who cannot more than tangentially recreate them as role models. To suggest why their work is so important, let me take another look at the contrast between dialectical and analogical thinking. David Tracy (1999) cites Paul Tillich (1957) as suggesting that the Protestant Principle, with its critical and prophetic impulse, which Tracy equates with the dialectical imagination, must always be complemented with Catholic substance. In other words, there must be something affirmed for there to be criticism of it. The tendency of modernity is to raise the idea of criticism to an absolute level, which makes some sense in a culture that is largely closed and dogmatic, but makes no sense in a culture which is already saturated with criticism from top to bottom.

It is, above all, substance that MacIntyre (1999) and Taylor (1999) give us, though both are fully capable of wielding the critical scalpel. Each has adopted quite a different tactic in his work, although both use the narrative of developing modernity as a frame for their arguments. Taylor (1999) has examined the emergence of modernity in the course of his magisterial *Sources of the Self* in order to discover what can be retrieved. This project followed a major book on Hegel as the thinker who made the most comprehensive early modern effort to recover substance in the face of criticism. *Sources of the Self* finds other figures, such as Herder and Humbolt, who can help us withstand the flood of negations, and he points in the end to the direction that his Marianist Lecture on Catholic modernity begins to develop. MacIntyre (1984) in *After Virtue*, surely one of the most seminal books of the last 50 years, engages in a much more drastic deconstruction of modernity than Taylor's more irenic project has entailed, but all in an effort to recover an Aristotelian/ Thomist substance to help us withstand the winds of nihilism, as his notion that our cultural choice boils down to Aristotle or Nietzsche indicates. In his subsequent books he has spelled out the sources from which, he argues, we may most usefully draw, and his most recent book, *Dependent Rational Animals* (1999), provides almost a primer of what a genuinely Aristotelian ethics would look like today.

Finding people like Taylor and MacIntyre to appoint in Catholic universities today will never be easy. And Marsden reminds us that even in universities with specific religious or indeed Catholic affiliation, there is no guarantee that scholars with the kind of explicit religious commitment that Taylor and MacIntyre express would be hired by departments whose self-conception is determined by disciplinary standards. Marsden suggests appointments funded from without the department, appointments we call at Berkeley "targets of opportunity," though persons with explicit religious convictions would regrettably not be such targets in my institution, as one way of bringing such people onto a campus. I am reminded that Nathan Pusey did have such an end in view when he brought Paul Tillich to Harvard in the 1950s as a University Professor, which meant he had the right to teach in any faculty. I audited his very well-attended undergraduate course on the Theology of Culture, which Morton White and some other professors vainly attacked as indoctrination and not worthy of inclusion in the undergraduate curriculum. Even when McGeorge Bundy brought Erik Erikson and David Riesman primarily to teach undergraduates without consulting the relevant departments, there was grumbling. So appointments from on high can be unsettling, though, in the examples I have given from Harvard, they turned out well in the eyes of most of the faculty and greatly to the benefit of the students. However it is brought about, I believe that only the presence of a number of scholars who exemplify the commitment to Catholic identity in dialogue with the modern world will make the project of an American Catholic university viable today. No amount of gimmicks can substitute for the presence of role models.

I want to talk a bit about curriculum, though tentatively, being aware of how many land mines there are in such a discussion. The contemporary university has become incoherent: in part because of the conflicting paradigms of what I would call positivism, postmodernism, and tradition, which MacIntyre (1990) described in *Three Rival Versions of Moral Enquiry*; in part because of the internal incoherence of the dominant positivist paradigm itself, where differentiation has proceeded apace with little accompanying effort at integration; and in part because of increasing external pressures on higher education. For postmodernists that is not a problem, since the only truth they recognize is incoherence; and for many faculty members it is not a problem because they have narrowed their world to their disciplinary sub-specialty and their colleagues in it with whom they can converse. The brunt of the incoherence falls on students, though some of them attempt to combat it by developing tribal loyalties to their majors.

The internal incoherence of the university is greatly exacerbated by the growing tendency to think of the university as the "education industry" whose major function is to prepare students for the job market. My coauthor Ann Swidler (1991) describes the institutional depletion which results:

> Many come to think of their education in purely instrumental terms, just like their work lives—an accumulation of credits toward a degree that will help them in the labor market. The idea that the college years allow time for the development of deeper understanding of history, cultures, and societies outside one's own, a deepened appreciation of one's own history and traditions, and reflection on the purpose and meaning of one's life in society—for appropriation of the enormous cultural endowment that is our birthright, won through generations of those who came before us—this conception of education is all but lost. (Bellah, Madsen, Sullivan, & Swidler, 1991)

Since students see no point in learning anything that isn't directly related to job possibilities, a course is only a means to the end of a degree that will lead to a good job. It is this that helps us understand an aspect of today's undergraduate education: for most students learning is not cumulative. What is learned in one course is likely to be quickly forgotten because, as one student put it, you have to "make room for the new stuff you need to know to do well in the next course."

Such external instrumentalization meets little resistance from the self-understanding of many of today's faculty members. Mark Taylor, speaking at Berkeley, recently said that when you ask undergraduates today what is the purpose of higher education, they reply, to learn critical thinking, and of course they got that idea from their teachers. Indeed college professors in institutions of liberal learning have long believed that one of their primary functions is to provide students with the critical tools which will allow them to rid their minds of the prejudices and superstitions they brought with them to college. But the prejudices and superstitions that students bring to the university today are seldom the product of the coherent but misguided worldview that the professors have in mind; instead it is the *disjecta membra* of postmodern culture. Thus when the practical nihilism of the students meets the practical nihilism of the faculty there is no ensuing Enlightenment but only a vacuum. What the students need above all is substance, metanarratives, that will give them some sense of who they are and what kind of world they live in. Only that counters the incoherence that surrounds them and gives them a context in which the skills of critical thinking make sense.

Let me consider some efforts to provide such substance, in the first instance, specifically Catholic substance. When I first heard about Catholic Studies Programs at Catholic universities, I was shocked— should not the Catholic identity permeate the whole curriculum? I have grown less shocked. In view of the inevitably secular nature of most of the curriculum at any contemporary university, a Catholic Studies Program, with links to many other parts of the university, is probably a very good idea. In such a program students move back and forth between classic texts and modern writers such as Taylor (1999) and MacIntyre (1999). Theology would be central, but the scope would, I hope, be comprehensive, and the analogical imagination would be cultivated without slighting the necessary correctives supplied by the dialectical imagination. Just to the extent that Thomism has lost the compulsory status that it enjoyed in the early 20th century, a free reappropriation of it could be refreshing, and the recognition that much that has taken its place is unconvincing and sobering. For students in such a program, learning would indeed be cumulative.

Recently, I have come across a related idea that I find most intriguing: a Classical Studies Program, which would be the revival of a traditional Jesuit education in a new form. The idea comes from Jerzy Axer, a professor at the University of Warsaw, who sees it not as a return to conservatism but as a contribution to education for democratic citizenship. Just to the degree that the ideas of classics, canons and Western Civilization have been trashed, we are liberated to see classical studies in an entirely new light. As Axer describes it:

> The purpose [of a concentration on classical studies including ancient languages] is the "suspension" of the pressure of historical experiences and the reduction of the pressure of mass culture stereotypes. The forgotten language of tradition takes us back to the common roots of Mediterranean civilization, and thereby counteracts the habits stemming from our bad and only too recent experiences. . . . Having

> thus cleared the arena and by way of initiating the Socratic
> educational dialogue, one could attempt jointly to recon-
> struct the world by resorting to universal signs. This sover-
> eign recreation anew of our civilization could awaken in
> the students naïve astonishment and delight—feelings
> which should be our fundamental goal and which are so
> difficult to arouse today. . . .
>
> We have left the smoldering ruins of Troy behind us, and
> our task resembles the mission of Aeneas, who was to
> revive it in another form and time. The meaning of such a
> mission can be formulated in the language of the classical
> tradition, and words which seem to be just commonplaces
> when heard and spoken in the squabbles and hubbub of
> daily life, regain their sense and authority thanks to the rec-
> ollections of their original contexts. If we wish to prepare
> society for becoming truly civic, and make citizens ready
> for participation in community instead of being outside
> observers, we must restore the conceptual apparatus, which
> endows meaning to the notion of Res Publica. (quoted in
> Katz, 1999, from World Wide Web)

The idea of a Classical Studies Program (which would have to be very
different from a professionalized classics program) as a kind of
anthropological journey that would illuminate our situation by its radical difference and lead to its possible renewal, is most intriguing and
one can see how it could overlap and interact with Catholic Studies,
for its very premise would be the revitalization of an analogical imagination.

I wish that I could see a way to break the stranglehold of disciplinary departments on our academic life, but I do not see any way
that would not jeopardize the academic standing of a university that
tried it and so undermine its capacity to continue. Nor do I think the
attempts at general education or core curriculum have done much to
change the incoherence of disciplinary division, though they are perhaps better than nothing. I am intrigued, however, by a suggestion
coming from the self-understanding of the early 19th century German
university where the faculty of philosophy was expected to function in
a dialectical relation with the more specialized faculties: "Each particular inquiry, each discipline, develops itself by interrogating its own
foundations with the aid of the faculty of philosophy. Thus, inquiry
passes from mere empirical practice to theoretical self-knowledge by

means of self-criticism" (Readings, 1999). While I doubt that departments of philosophy today would see themselves as either qualified or interested in such an endeavor, I think, especially in a Catholic university of moderate size, the faculty itself might decide to embark on such a task of disciplinary self-interrogation; each department would examine its historical origins and the present understandings of its purpose, as well as its boundary relations with other disciplines and its possible blind spots. I suspect a close look at the actual practices going on in the various fields, including the natural sciences, might yield more analogies than we might expect (Latour, 1994). A process of mutual self-interrogation might bring some greater understanding of the relationship of the parts to the whole. I cannot guarantee that it might not just reveal the true extent of the underlying chaos, but I think it is worth a try.

Finally I can only allude to what may be the most important thing of all: the conception of the Catholic university as a worshipping community. I believe the Eucharist is the heart of our common life and the celebration of Mass ought to be at the center of a Catholic university. It is there that the analogical imagination takes over our consciousness and makes all things real. (I am reminded of John Milbank's comment that ". . . outside liturgy, there can be no meaning.") But we are beyond the stage of coercion. Here I think we, and I include priests and laity, faculty and students, must engage in a complex effort of *persuasion* as to why a Catholic presence in the university and in our lives makes sense. The last chapter of Hans Joas's (2000) book that I mentioned earlier is on reconciling the right and the good. The right necessarily always involves constraint; laws must be enforced. But we are drawn to the good by love. Joas (2000) quotes Goethe as saying, "One knows nothing save what one loves, and the deeper and more complete that knowledge, the stronger and livelier must be one's love." That applies first of all to the love and knowledge of God, which we express above all in prayer and worship, but it applies to the whole of our educational life. The love of God and of all the forms of good that overflow from God must be at the heart of any university that would call itself Christian or Catholic.

REFERENCES

Bellah, R., (Ed.). (1985). *Habits of the Heart: Individualism and Commitment in American Life.* Berkeley, CA: University of California Press.

Bellah, R., Madsen, R., Sullivan, W. M., & Swidler, A. (1991). *The Good Society.* New York: Random House.

Bellows, H. W. (1859). "The suspense of faith." In C. Wright (Ed.). (1989), *Walking Together: Polity and Participation in Unitarian and Universalist Churches.* Boston: Skinner House.

Greely, A. (2000). *The Catholic Imagination.* Berkely, CA: University of California Press.

Gustafson, J. M. (1983). *Ethics from a Theocentric Perspective.* Chicago: University of Chicago Press.

Heft, J. L. (Ed.). (1999). *A Catholic Modernity?* Oxford, England: Oxford University Press.

Joas, H. (2000). *The Genesis of Values.* New York: Polty Press.

Katz, S. N. (1999). "Can liberal education cope?" Retrieved from the World Wide Web: http://www.wws.princeton.edu/~snkatz/papers/ag/sp.html.

Kung, H. (1995). *Christianity: Essence, History, and Future.* New York: Continuum.

Latour, B. (1994). *We Have Never Been Modern.* Cambridge, MA: Harvard University Press.

MacIntyre, A. C. (1984). *After Virtue: A Study in Moral Theory.* Notre Dame, IN: University of Notre Dame Press.

MacIntyre, A. C. (1990). *Three Rival Versions of Moral Inquiry.* Notre Dame, IN: University of Notre Dame Press.

MacIntyre, A. C. (1999). "Dependent Rational Animals." Chicago: Open Court.

Marsden, G. (1994). *The Soul of the American University: From Protestant Establishment to Established Non-Belief.* Oxford, England: Oxford University Press.

Niebuhr, H. R. (1970). *Radical Monotheism and Western Culture.* New York: Harper Torchbooks.

Readings, W. (1999). In S. N. Katz, "Can liberal education cope?" Retrieved from the World Wide Web: http://www.wws.prince ton.edu/~snkatz/papers/ag/sp.html.

Taylor, C. (1999). Source of the self. In J. L. Heft (Ed.), *A Catholic Modernity? Charles Taylor's Marianist Award Lecture, With Responses.* England: Oxford University Press.

Tillich, P. (1957). *The Protestant Era* (J. L. Adams, Trans.). Chicago: University of Chicago Press.

Tracy, D. (1981). *The Analogical Imagination.* New York: Crossroad.

The Catholic Sacramental Imagination

Doris Donnelly

> Spiritual versus material, sacred versus profane, supernatu-
> ral versus natural–such were for centuries the only accept-
> ed, the only understandable moulds and categories of reli-
> gious thought and experience . . . (but) nowhere in the
> Bible do we find the dichotomies which for us are the self-
> evident framework for all approaches to religion. In the
> Bible the food that people eat, the world of which they
> must partake in order to live, is given to them by God, and
> it is given as communion with God.
>
> . . . the original sin is not primarily that someone "dis-
> obeyed" God; the sin is that someone ceased to see all of
> life dependent on the whole world as sacrament of com-
> munion with God.

(Schmemman, 1973)

I t seems to me that the theme of the President's Institute—the Catholic sacramental imagination—is a perfect fit for faculty exploration at Catholic universities. In the first place, the Catholic imagination is part of the way we have become inculturated at Catholic and particularly Jesuit institutions. Our orientation into what was important to Ignatius of Loyola is a high degree of comfort with the world and the way the world reveals God. Catholic sacramental imagination is wrapped up in the world we know and in which we live.

It is true that at the beginning of his spiritual journey, Ignatius renounced the world and considered it an impediment to his search for God. But disdain gave way to embrace when the phrase "finding God in all things" became a shorthand for Ignatian spirituality. It is a fundamental Ignatian theme. Of course, coming full circle from loathing to loving the world has not been an isolated episode in Christian conversion stories, but Ignatius provides a few unique variations on the theme. For example, the world is not only the place where God is to be found, it is also the place where God is to be served. We are all stewards of that legacy of service through education, believing as we

49

do that minds and bodies, or to paraphrase Alexander Schememann, the spiritual and the material—the supernatural and the natural—are not adversaries but friends.

There is a second reason why the theme of the Catholic sacramental imagination is apt for university faculty reflection. It is a theme congenial to educators who ply their trade by encouraging critical thinking and by suggesting to students that what is obvious to the naked eye is usually not all there is to see. We operate on an, often subversive assumption, that people, events, and things are capable of mediating far more than what we see on the outside, in contrast to the "what you see is what you get" mentality guiding much of life around us. I am reminded in this context of a charming story told by theologian Balthasar Fischer (1989) of an encounter with a young child who was enchanted by fairy tales:

> "Are these stories true?" he gently teased.
> The little girl pondered the question seriously.
> "On the outside no, but on the inside yes," she answered.

The Catholic sacramental imagination knows that the little girl's reply was accurate: there is often more to things, events, and people than what we see on the surface. I am a teacher—by profession a theologian—who has specialized in sacramental theology, and, more specifically, in the areas of forgiveness and reconciliation, during my academic career. By commitment, disposition, inclination, and intentional choice, I am a Catholic. Because of my Catholic heritage, my life as teacher, daughter, wife, mother, friend, theologian, and colleague enables me to live comfortably in the world of metaphors, signs, symbols, and sacraments. Because of that upbringing, I think and have understood all my life Philip Wheelwright's (1982) distinction between steno symbols and tensive symbols. Like Balthasar Fischer's niece, I relate instinctively to tensive symbols that provide a give-and-take involvement in what is unsaid and unseen, knowing that further revelation often comes from unexpected sources and in ways we cannot anticipate. Steno symbols—rational, direct, unambiguous—fall prey to a flatminded literalism that, to my mind, subverts education by limiting the imagination. The steno symbol for red might be danger; but it takes thinking in the tensive mode to include red's possibilities as the color of charity, martyrdom, hell, love, old theatre seats, blood, valentines, fire, paprika, rubies, and the cardinals of the Roman Catholic Church (Theroux, 1994).

As a university professor, I value insight from my students and encourage critical thinking and mastery of the material. In David Tracy's (1981) terminology, I honor, as you do, the dialectical imagination. But does not our authority in the classroom rest on both knowing the facts as well as knowing, through the creative and intuitive analogical imagination, uncharted terrain to be explored and unexpected discoveries to be made? It does for me, and so I hold—rather stubbornly in fact—that the dialectic imagination needs to exist and be valued alongside the analogical imagination.

As a theologian, I have seen a major evolution in sacramental theology in recent years that follows the intuition of the analogical imagination. One facet of that evolution has to do with simple numbers. In the days before the Second Vatican Council, the catechisms taught seven sacraments: baptism, Eucharist, confirmation, penance, holy orders, marriage, and anointing of the sick. Little, if any, distinction was made among them. Around the time of Vatican II we still recognized seven sacraments but two of these—baptism and Eucharist—were designated as major sacraments and five were designated as minor ones (Congar, 1967). Baptism and Eucharist were awarded their special status, since they more closely and clearly revealed the mysteries connected with the dying and rising of Christ.

A second facet of the sacraments' evolution had to do with an extended definition of sacrament. Once defined as an outward sign of inward grace, sacrament is now understood as a symbol that participates in the reality of the life, death, and resurrection of Jesus Christ and effects that reality, i.e., makes it happen. Faith, of course, is a prerequisite to the sacramental imagination, since sacraments are not acts of magic. With faith we are able to identify many more things than we might once have thought of as sacraments. The Church, for example, is a sacrament insofar as it participates in the reality of Christ and effects that reality. And certainly Jesus is a sacrament since he, above all, is transparently related to the one he addresses as "Father," and his presence more directly discloses the reality of God (Rahner, 1963).

In this context it could be suggested that we are each sacraments or signs of God's presence when we allow God to be visible through what we say and do. As husbands, wives, coworkers, friends, and children, we all have opportunities to be transparent to the generosity, compassion, forgiveness, understanding, and gift of self that was Christ's way of being in the world. Of course, we are also free to do the opposite—to be countersigns of Christ's presence—and to that extent the world is diminished.

A third facet of sacramental theology has to do with a heightened awareness of the strength of signs to disclose the beyond. While it may well be true that Vatican II reaffirmed the world as the place where God lives, is found, shared, known, loved, or denied, and where symbols have the power to connect to God's presence and activity, the temptation remains to domesticate and literalize them. The world is likewise filled with metaphors capable of disclosing the Divine, but some of these metaphors are routinely rendered lifeless and disconnected.

Metaphors are not supposed to function that way. Gail Ramshaw (2000) writes that they are like firecrackers, exploding and sending sparks that connect with other sparks and shed fresh light on what we might not have seen before. Once seen, they reinforce a vision powerful enough to knock our socks off.

The Eucharist, for example, invites us to a gathering where a story is told and told again with lifegiving potential. The story is complemented by a ritual where symbols are let loose in our imaginations and lives. Though some might identify bread and wine as those symbols, the truth is that symbols and metaphors are not nouns but verbs. Thus, at the Eucharistic ritual, the symbols are not bread and wine, but rather eating from one loaf and drinking from one cup. The symbol is not that we are isolated, separate members of a club but rather that we are interconnected sharers and members of one body and community, larger than the sum of its parts (Mitchell, 1977).

As another example, reducing the symbolism of baptism to water (a noun) instead of being immersed in water (a verb) does not convey the death by drowning and the new life that is, or needs to be, disclosed in that sacrament. Trickling little drops of water on a person's head does not do justice to the sacrament's potential to reveal new life.

Of course, what should be growing obvious is that while the physical world is capable of revealing the divine, that revelation is often indirect and limited and ambiguous, while many of us yearn for revelation that is direct, unlimited, and unambiguous. What helps in the eventual progressive disclosure of sacramental symbolism is familiarity with the world outside the official religious sphere—for example, in the arts (in poetry, music, and painting)—and in subjects we teach, the issues we raise in the classroom, and the discoveries we make there as well. Sometimes, and maybe it is most often, those signs of grace, of God's presence in the world, are found in the ordinary.

Paying attention to the ordinary and giving it time to disclose the divine is not an easy assignment, but one person who measures up to the task is the writer Kathleen Norris. In her essay "Sea Change" (1993) she offers a unique contribution to the sacramental imagination. In this essay, the sea change she writes about is her move from New York City to western South Dakota—a move of the heart, gut, and perspective as much as of geographical distance. In fact, mileage on the odometer is probably the least adequate in measuring the change that took place for her.

In a culture that prizes the different, the new, and the stimuli, Kathleen Norris prefers the slow lane. She lives comfortably as a woman of the 21st century in this freely chosen place away from the buzz and the hype that keep many functioning. Norris compares living in South Dakota to living in a monastery, and since she is familiar with both forms, as an affiliate of the Benedictine Order as well as a bona fide citizen of South Dakota, she probably knows what she's talking about. Living in South Dakota, she says, works best when one knows the options, when one survives a "testing" as new recruits do in a monastery, and then makes a free choice. At first, one experiences some disorientation and at times an overwhelming sense of loneliness; nothing fast and noisy exists to distract from what lies before one's eyes—a fat-faced moon rising above the prairie, ranches of several thousand acres, and a spectacularly desolate moonscape of sagebrush (Norris, 1993). It is in this setting that monotony and repetition tested Norris and found her a willing candidate for a conversion which enabled her to focus not only on what lay in front of her but also on what lay within her. She found, in the inhospitable bareness of South Dakota, a place, like a monastery, where it was impossible to hide out and to escape the demands of life. Conversely, it became for her a place where huge doses of patience and fidelity were tested and then rewarded with insight and growth. She witnessed over and over again that through monotony, in a strange paradoxical way, the presence of God was disclosed and came with a personal uncluttered experience of the transcendent.

For educators, Kathleen Norris offers a challenge. There are few South Dakotas in education these days. CNN, the Internet, e-mail, classroom technology, the information superhighway, and global travel are capable of placing every college and university in the fast lane. Students can access thousands of pages of information quickly and efficiently, and, if they are motivated, they can read, summarize, and submit this same information in papers and class presentations. The challenge for educators, then, is to offer a contemplative perspective—a pause from accumulation to simplicity—an invitation to slow down and allow what lies before them to disclose all that is there beneath the surface if they (and we) only take time to notice.

There is a countercultural feel to this style of teaching and learning as we are introduced almost daily to new offerings in cyber-education. And surely there is place for it. What Kathleen Norris offers is not an either-or but a corrective to the overemphasis on the new, the different, and the fashionable. Hers is a gentle suggestion that we not lose sight that skin deep is not enough; hers is an offer that what lies beneath is enough to ignite us in ways we never could have imagined. What lies above—the visible—and what lies beneath and needs to be plumbed—combine to expose the Catholic sacramental imagination.

Furthermore, Norris writes about a formation process necessary in the monastic life and by extension in the contemplative life in any slow lane: "One must make an informed rejection of any other way of life and also undergo a period of formation" (Norris, 1993, p. 153). She gives us pause to consider that probing underneath texts in history, or mathematical formulae, or laboratory experiments, renaissance dramas, or contemporary poetry is not automatic. The novices, our students, need guides who have been there, who have done some probing beneath the surface on their own before they can accompany others, and who are willing to mentor and act as "formation directors" for students struggling to find their own "home" and path. For Norris, contemplation and prayer play a part in this mentorship and formation. She echoes a familiar Ignatian theme: the teacher must model not only competency and scholarship but also a style of life where virtue is alive and well.

In some ways, Brian Doyle (1999) offers an example of what attention to the sacramental imagination looks like if one follows the advice of Kathleen Norris. His essay, "Filled with Grace," is a poignant story about his son who was born missing a chamber in his heart. In the background is the story of André Dubus, who inspired Doyle's essay. Dubus ". . . ran after grace, without his legs, having lost them on a highway one hot summer night, in the same instant that he shoved a young woman out of the way of the speeding car that sent him reeling into a wheelchair for the rest of his life" (Doyle, 1999, p. 46). Doyle, like Dubus, lived through a dark night of his own. He writes of the grace that sustained him through the operations on his infant son, the fear in his own body that he might lose his child, and the need to touch that little body of his son because, in the words of Dubus: "Without touch, God is a monologue, an idea, a philosophy. He must touch and be touched . . . in the instant of the touch there is no place for thinking, for talking: the silent touch affirms all that, and goes deeper: it affirms the mysteries of love and mortality" (Doyle, 1999, p. 49).

Doyle's focus on the body is very much part of the sacramental imagination. When the incarnation of Jesus is dislocated (as it often is) into a mystical, otherworldly sphere of spirit disembodied, the Good News is mocked and so is the sacramentality and holiness of the body. We need our bodies to express who we are. We need the body of Jesus in order to understand, however imperfectly, who God is. Doyle reminds us that Jesus took flesh, and by taking it blessed it and made it a place where intense grace can come through anyone's body. As a result of that conviction, he can experience and then write about grace this way:

> When have I been filled with grace? One time above all others, when my son was under ether. He was born with a broken heart, an incomplete heart, part of a heart. Not enough to keep him alive. Twice doctors cut him open and stilled his heart and cut into it. Twice I waited and raged and chewed my fingers until they bled. . . . Yet out of the dark came my wife's hand like a hawk, and I believe to this hour, that when she touched me I received pure grace. She woke me, saved me, not for the first time, not for the last. (Doyle, 1999, p. 48)

If nothing else, Brian Doyle's essay reminds us that real things and real people, ordinary though they may be, are the vehicles of disclosing grace simply and intensely.

Anne Sexton is still another person whose writing discloses the sacramental imagination at work. She is often explicit about the connections between the material universe and the spiritual. Her writing is at the same time passionate and personal. It is also disturbing, because her intimacy with the divine is so severe and unconventional. In her poems, she sees God alternately as an island, a poker player, a cigar smoker, and at the same time profoundly involved in her life. This intimacy is either unnerving or inviting, depending on one's point of view.

Take, for example, her poem "The Earth" (Sexton, 1981, pp. 431–432):

> God loafs around heaven
> without a shape
> but He would like to smoke His cigar
> or bite His fingernails
> and so forth.
>
> God owns heaven
> but He craves the earth,
> the earth with its little sleepy caves,
> its bird resting at the kitchen window,
> even its murders lined up like broken chairs,
> even its writers digging into their souls
> with jackhammers,
> even its hucksters selling their animals
> for gold,
> even its babies sniffing for their music,
>
> the farm house, white as a bone,
> sitting in the lap of its corn,
> even the statue holding up its widowed life,
> even the ocean with its cupful of students,
> but most of all He envies the bodies,
> He who has no body.
>
> The eyes, opening and shutting like keyholes
> and never forgetting, recording by thousands,
> the skull with its brain like eels –
> the tablet of the world –
> the bones and their joints
> that build and break for any trick,

the genitals,
the ballast of the eternal,
and the heart, of course,
that swallows the tides
and spits them out cleansed.
He does not envy the soul so much.
He is all soul
but He would like to house it in a body
and come down
and give it a bath
now and then.

For Sexton, God is near, approachable, connected with creation, and waiting to be found in the ordinary.

How ordinary? Her poem "Welcome Morning" (Sexton, 1981, pp. 431–432) captures both the presence of God in simple daily happenings and also acknowledges the reality that because the possibilities come in such ordinary places they are too frequently missed. She tells it this way:

There is joy
in all
in the hair I brush each morning,
in the Cannon towel, newly washed,
that I rub my body with each morning,
in the chapel of eggs I cook
each morning,
in the outcry from the kettle
that heats my coffee
each morning,
in the spoon and the chair
that cry "hello there, Anne,"
each morning,
in the godhead of the table
that I set my silver, plate, cup upon
each morning.

All this is God,
right here in my pea green house
each morning
and I mean,
though often forget
to give thanks,

to faint down by the kitchen table
in a prayer of rejoicing
as the holy birds at the kitchen window
peck into their marriage of seeds.

So while I think of it,
let me paint a thank-you on my palm
for this God, this laughter of the morning,
lest it go unspoken.

The Joy that isn't shared, I've heard,
dies young.

Although he may not have had Cannon towels, eggs, or ket-
tles in mind, Avery Dulles (1980), for one, has written that everything
has the potential to disclose the reality of God and thus factor in the
sacramental imagination. Anne Sexton reinforces his certitude. God *is*
here, she says. God is present in what may seem to be insignificant
moments, and that probably has a lot to do with why we miss the
epiphanies all around us. God is even in the monotony and/or stress of
our work. In her poem "Frenzy," (Sexton, 1981) she unsettles those of
us who want to compartmentalize our work as not "with" God and
buoys those of us who glimpse the connection and grasp, like a life
preserver, the map she offers:

I am not lazy.
I am on the amphetamine of the soul.
I am, each day,
typing out the God
my typewriter believes in.
Very quick. Very intense,
Like a wolf at a live heart.

Sexton describes her work as a search for God. Energized and
in full pursuit, she is far from lazy and has every reason to expect the
windows of heaven will remain open and will reward her:

Oh angels,
keep the windows open
so that I may reach in
and steal each object,

objects that tell me the sea is not dying,
objects that tell me the dirt has a life-wish,
that the Christ who walked for me,
walked on true ground
and that this frenzy,
like bees stinging the heart all morning,
will keep the angels
with their windows open,
wide as an English bathtub. (Sexton, 1981, p. 466)

So there seems to be hope for ordinary people to find God in ordinary ways and in ordinary places, if we would but look and look deeply. That hope is unraveled and then raveled up again (Sexton does not give away answers but rather seduces us to navigate our own pathway to God). Here is her poem "Snow":

Snow
blessed snow,
comes out of the sky
liked bleached flies.
The ground is no longer naked.
The ground has on its clothes.
The trees poke out of sheets
and each branch wears the sock of God.

There is hope.
There is hope everywhere.
I bite it.
Someone once said:
Don't bite till you know

if it's bread or stone.
What I bite is all bread,
Rising, yeasty as a cloud.

There is hope.
There is hope everywhere.
Today God gives milk
and I have the pail. (Sexton, 1981, p. 467)

There is hope everywhere, even when we do not see "bleached flies" and branches wearing the "sock of God," even when violence and tragedy are part of the landscape. Not only does God provide hope, but the hope given us is not stingy but prodigal. Why else, when God gives milk, would she carry a pail and not a tea cup or a thimble to catch it as it flows into her life?

And our lives? Is there hope for us as well? Does the sacramental imagination and contact with the physical universe allow us to see that we are touching holy ground all the time? And if the sacramental imagination does this, where, exactly, do we find hope? Given Anne Sexton's certainty, we cannot assume that these are rhetorical questions. Just the opposite. She and Kathleen Norris and Brian Doyle are waiting for an answer. Your answer.

With them in mind, I invite you to spend some time in the slow lane on the contemplative track and to tell us, if you like, where *you* find hope and where God has entered your hands. I welcome the fruits of the searching and finding of the members of the President's Institute 2000 and offer as souvenirs five verifications that milk is plentiful at Loyola Marymount University and everyone, it seems, is carrying a pail to contain it:

Where Do I Find Hope?

When I was young, alert, eager
I could see God
in everything from snails to shooting stars.
My voice was quick to praise
the Loving God painting on the window
of the world
and beckoning me beyond the glass
to Heaven.

Now that I am old I wonder
if I am speaking to the point
hesitant that I may misplace my keys.
Is God hiding from me?
I see snails and shooting stars through smudged
glasses.
My voice quivers as I ask where God is.
I rub the pane on which God paints.
And, yes, ever so dimly there is God,
Moving my hand and helping me draw.
                    By Herbert Ryan S.J. (2000)

The Family Plot

November.
At the cemetery on the edge of the prairie
    we are standing together
        at the opening of our father's grave.
From the new-plowed field of stubbled grain
    whirlwinds of rich dark earth blow into
        tiny tornadoes among the stones.
    Honore.
    Maria.
    Evelyn.
    Lois.
        Father.
        Mother.
        Two wives.

My brother—the clown—is weeping inconsolably.

My brother—the serious one—looks across the
    deep space and smiles at me.
        He widens his hands.
He has paced off the places left in the family plot.
    ("I'm not sure," he said, laughing,
        "that there is room enough for you.")

My sister—the good daughter—who has sat for
hours,
    who has driven for miles, week after week,
        is far away.
Her sad brown eyes fix on the
    Grain elevator in the distance, beyond the
plowed field.
("He said they had come for him. They waited,
    at the foot of the bed.")

    Honore.
    Maria.
    Evelyn.

Lois.

Father.
Mother.
Two wives.

On the way back to the motel
        in the town that once was home,
                we laugh and tell stories.

"Sharon, you have to lose a few pounds,"
        says my brother the clown, "if
                you're going to fit in that little
space."

"*Kindje,*" my sister says, in a voice that sounds
        so much like Grandma's, "It's okay.
                You're just right. Nice and fat!"

My serious brother begins to weep inconsolably.

"*Kindje,*" I say to him, "it's all right.
        There is room enough for both of us."
                                By Sharon Locy (2000)

(Julius E. Locy died Nov. 3, 1999; he is buried in St.
Edward's cemetery in Minneota, Minnesota, beside
his mother and father, Maria and Honore, and
between his two wives, Evelyn and Lois.)

                    Prodigal Hands

I remember my father's hands:
Large-boned, red and freckled.
Irish hands.
He dug in the garden, scooping the dirt
and packing it flat around fragile flowers.
And one terrible night, he beat my brother
who was five.
Quick-handed cracks and slaps.

That night when my father knelt to pray
his hands covered his face for
a long quiet moment.
Then he crossed himself with a swift hand.
Sometimes, from behind, his firm hands dropped

on my shoulders with a steering weight.
He taught the firm handshake, a tight grip.

II

I remember my son's hands:
Fingers like flower stem.
We taught him to reach around
our necks, to hold us gently.
His hands grew large, almost
clumsy for his teenage body.
No one ever told him that men don't
hold men.
Until that Christmas Eve when
my father came through the door.
My son's hands reached for him,
but a solitary hand thrust out
backed by a warning voice:
"Here. I'm a handshake kind of guy."

III

O, hands of my prodigal life!
Am I the son who still trudges
up a rocky hill, my stinking clothes
in tatters, penniless and penitent,
only to find a solitary handshake?

Or am I the waiting father of open arms,
both hands reaching, then pulling
sagging shoulders toward me and
gently, so gently, folding that face
Into ourselves?

                    By Scott Wood (2000)

Godless Country

Once upon a time
there was a country
a country where people knew no God
And people lived, their sinful lives
and they used happily, their trivial days
learning to love each other in peace

But one day, everything has changed around
and people accepted God into their lives
but not too long, after this joyful act
they killed, tortured, and raped one another

Many of them have terribly perished
during the bloodbath that lasted too long
and how could this be, one may ask
Is there a hope for those who survived?

There is a mystery in the workings of God
There is a hope in the garden of the Lord

There will be light,
but only for those,
who stick around,
for long enough

By Mladen Milicevic (2000)

Bede

The old man flexes his
fingers,
Tired from writing
the Word of God.
The script so precise yet delicate,
the tracery so fine.
The words float across the vellum
full of grace, heavy with wonder.
He sighs, stretches, gazes

at his age spotted hands.
How long can these
fingers
grasp the quill, fashion the shapes
of the letters?
Life is on the page, hope, salvation.
There is much to write.
The old man takes up the quill,
his fingers again grasping,
guiding, putting the Light
on the parchment,
Light
Truth
Hope.

By Jane Crawford (2000)

REFERENCES

Congar, Y., O.P. (1967). "The notion of 'major' or 'principal' sacraments." *Concilium, 31*, 21–32.

Doyle, B. (1999, Autumn). "Filled with grace." *Notre Dame Magazine*, 46–49.

Dulles, A. (1980, March). "The symbolic structure of revelation." *Theological Studies, 41*, 51–70.

Fischer, B. (1989). In J. McKenna, "Symbol and reality: Some anthropological considerations." *Worship, 65* (1), 2–27.

McKenna, J. (1989, January). "Symbol and reality: Some anthropological considerations." *Worship, 65*, (1), 2–27.

Mitchell, N. (1977, February). "Symbols are actions, not objects – New directions for an old problem." *Living Worship, 13*, (2), 1–2.

Norris, K. (1993). "Sea Change." In *Dakota: A Spiritual Geography* (pp. 145–153). Boston, MA: Houghton Mifflin Company.

Rahner, K., S.J. (1963). *The Church and the Sacraments*. (W.J. O'Hara, Trans.). New York, NY: Herder and Herder.

Rahner, K., S.J. (1966). "The theology of the symbol." In *Theological Investigations IV* (pp. 221–252). Baltimore, MD: Helicon Press.

Ramshaw, G. (2000, January). *The Valley of Dry Metaphors*. Unpublished President's Address at the North American Academy of Liturgy Meeting, Tampa, FL.

Schmemman, A. (1973). *For the Life of the World: Sacraments and Orthodoxy*. Crestwood, NY: St. Vladmir's Seminary Press.

Sexton, A. (1981). "The earth." In *Complete Poems* (pp. 431–432). Boston, MA: Houghton Mifflin Company.

Theroux, A. (1994). *Primary Colors*. New York, NY: Henry Holt and Company.

Tracy, D. (1981). *The Analogical Imagination*. New York, NY: Crossroad.

Wheelwright, P. E. (1982). *The Burning Fountain: A Study in the Language of Symbolism*. Gloucester, MA: P. Smith.

The Genesis Of Apocalypse:
Religious Roots of Coppola's Vietnam Epic

Richard Blake, S.J.

In its ten-year script development *Apocalypse Now* passed through many transformations. In the reflections that follow, I hope to offer a plausible rationale for the consistent trajectory of the successive stages in the script that eventually reached its audience as a finished product in the summer of 1979. Beginning in 1975 Francis Coppola continually rewrote the John Milius script of 1969, and in the process of editing, introduced the voice-over narration by Michael Herr. During this lengthy production period, Coppola often found himself forced into changes by events he could neither anticipate nor control. Even so, I would like to propose the notion that, in putting together the final version that eventually reached the public, he was guided, consciously or not, by a particularly Catholic way of interpreting the moral universe in which his characters seek some form of redemption. As a result, he continually moved the film away from the ideology of John Milius, who identifies himself as a Zen fascist, and closer to its conceptual roots in its ultimate source material, *Heart of Darkness* (Conrad, 1988), an 1899 novella by Joseph Conrad (1857–1924).

Conrad grew up in the Catholic tradition in Poland, but in 1874 he moved to France and what he hoped would be a life of seafaring. Four years later he shipped aboard a British merchant vessel and gradually assumed an English identity. Although not an active Catholic through most of his adult life, Conrad claims to have remained a believer and was buried with the rites of the Catholic Church (Lester, 1988). Coppola, for his part, through his life and his films has shown great fondness for his Italian heritage, which has been inextricably intertwined with Catholic traditions and rituals for centuries. Through their religious roots the two artists show a remarkable affinity.

The Conscience of Colonialism

Ostensibly *Heart of Darkness* is Conrad's indictment of the age of colonialism, especially as he experienced it in Africa. As we read the novel today, however, his interests clearly involve more than a critique of the faltering imperial structures of the 19th century. Of much greater concern is his analysis of the effect of an evil, corrupt world on its seemingly neutral inhabitants. His protagonist, Charlie Marlow, travels up the Congo river to retrieve Mr. Kurtz, an agent of a Belgian trading company who has been extraordinarily successful in collecting ivory for export to Europe. Kurtz's effectiveness is largely due to his ability to recruit and intimidate the local tribespeople, who treat him with respect bordering on worship. In recent years, however, his productivity has diminished, and the company suspects that he has been amassing a vast personal treasure for himself rather than for his employers. He may be sick, or mad or possibly even dead. The board wants an explanation, and it wants Kurtz removed from his station and brought back to the home office in Belgium. Marlow locates Kurtz, but finds him quite ill. Marlow insists on bringing him out, but Kurtz resists and dies on the river boat on his way back to the Central Station.

During his journey, Marlow realizes that, as a European and an employee of the trading company, he too is part of the evil system. Albert Guerard (1965) argues persuasively that the core of the novel is Marlow's discovery of his own inner life, rather than a study of Kurtz's immersion in evil. Years later, Marlow makes peace with his past by recounting the story to four fellow Englishmen as they wait for the tide to carry them out of the Thames estuary. His inclusion of the gruesome details of colonial life in the Congo clearly indicates that, in retrospect, he recognizes the evil for what it was. The narrative becomes his confession. He begins with an incident on his initial journey to the Congo. As he sailed down the coast of Africa, Marlow recalls, he observed a French gunboat pointlessly lobbing shells into the dense African forest, as though its random, destructive violence could effect any change on the continent. As he travels up the Congo itself, he witnesses the folly of colonial enterprises and the dehumanizing consequences for those Europeans who try to establish them as well as for the Africans who endure them. White accountants wear immaculate starched collars on their shirts, while black African workers and prisoners wear chains eerily reminiscent of the slave trade of an earlier era.

Kurtz represents the extreme form of colonial exploitation, as represented by the shrunken heads that decorate his compound. In the report he has been preparing for the International Society for the Suppression of Savage Customs, Kurtz adds a postscript: "Exterminate all the brutes" (Conrad, 1988, p. 51). Kurtz's physical sickness reflects the moral sickness Marlow discovers in the social structures. Both lead only to death. Furthermore, Kurtz has regressed into a primitive and predatory state, and rather than return to civilization with Marlow, he tries to crawl deeper into the forest, on all fours, like a hunted animal. Marlow is an observer, but as he acknowledges, a participant observer. He cannot separate himself from the evil he observes.

As the final phase of his narration, Marlow adds a coda to the story of his African adventure. He tells his shipmates of visiting Kurtz's fiancée soon after his return to Europe. When she asks about his last words, Marlow perpetuates a romantic lie. He tells her that Kurtz died repeating her name. He cannot tell her that he died whispering, "The horror! The horror!" a splendidly terrifying but ambiguous comment on his life and on the world that people like him had created (Watt, 1979). When Marlow finally gives Kurtz's report to a representative of the company, possibly a solicitor, he first tears out the scribbled comment "Exterminate all the brutes." Neither fiancée nor company representative, any more than the European population at large, could face those brutal realities, nor did Marlow, at first, have the courage even to try to relay the truth. Only in the framing story, occurring some years after the event, could he unveil the barbarity he had observed in the Congo. For Marlow the shipboard narrative becomes a form of confession, a particularly Catholic means of purifying the soul of past guilt.

Conrad's reflections on the nature of this evil, as embodied in Kurtz's exercise of colonial power, are shaped by an identifiably Catholic set of assumptions. With its emphasis on community, the "communion of saints," the Catholic imagination readily sees humankind as striving toward heaven in a world marred by a form of universal evil that traces its mythic roots back to the original sin in Adam's fall from paradise. Those on earth, like Marlow, are still in a pilgrim state striving for salvation; those in Purgatory are saved but now await final purification before receiving their final reward; only those in heaven constitute that part of the "communion" that is unambiguously blessed. By his actions in this pilgrim phase of his life Kurtz has isolated himself physically and morally. Thus he faces damnation, the

horror" that he sees at the moment of his death when his exclusion
from the communion of saints is irrevocably ratified.

Conrad does not charge Charlie Marlow with any particular
act of sinfulness in his earlier life. Marlow describes himself as merely a sailor looking for work and seizing the opportunity to visit the
Congo, a region that excited his curiosity even as a boy (Conrad,
1988). However, by simply being part of the human family that is universally stained with primal sin, Marlow is in fact a sinner. By observ-
ing the varied manifestations of human evil during his voyage, especially the insane cruelty and greed of Mr. Kurtz and its ultimate consequences, Marlow recognizes himself as another Kurtz, a pilgrim
touched by the sin of the world who may succumb to it as Kurtz has.
As Kurtz nears death, Marlow reflects:

> But his [Kurtz's] soul was mad. Being alone in the wilder-
> ness, it had looked within itself and, by heavens I tell you,
> it had gone mad. I had—for my sins, I suppose—to go
> through the ordeal of looking into it myself. (Conrad, 1988,
> p. 65)

At the least Marlow sees Kurtz as precedent for himself, and perhaps
he even fears that Kurtz is an alter ego. Isolated as he was from the
restraints of civilization, Kurtz embraced his dark side and gave it free
rein (Watt, 1979). Marlow recognizes this in Kurtz, and with a terror
that threatens madness, realizes that his own heart, no less than
Kurtz's, harbors an unspeakable darkness held in check by the frailest
of social conventions. Like Kurtz, he could fall off the edge into madness.

This horrifying examination of conscience leads directly to
Marlow's belated confession to his traveling companions on the ship
in the Thames estuary. Marlow indeed felt that he had traveled to the
edge of hell in his pursuit of Kurtz. Conrad describes the night on
which Kurtz left the boat and crawled into the jungle on all fours as
infernal: fires blazing in the dark, incessant drums, figures lurking in
the shadows, a mysterious priest with antlers like Satanic horns fas-
tened to his head. Marlow comments:

> What made this emotion [terror] so overpowering was—
> how shall I define it—the moral shock I received, as if
> something altogether monstrous, intolerable to thought and

odious to the soul had been thrust upon me unexpectedly. (Conrad, 1988, p. 63)

Marlow even finds relief when he manages to relocate his fear in some actual possibility, like an imminent massacre. He plunges into the infernal darkness after Kurtz, and moves through the night with the ease of a skilled hunter or animal "chuckling to [him]self" (p. 64). Marlow faced the spell of "forgotten and brutal instincts," but prevailed over the darkness of the forest and returned with Kurtz to the boat, an image of civilization.

They set off down river together, blasting the steam whistle to frighten away Kurtz's primitive, demonic, worshippers. While Marlow has the strength to return to civilization, Kurtz dies on the first day of the journey. Marlow has not yet fallen off the edge, but Kurtz had already chosen darkness and could never return. Through Kurtz's death Marlow gains freedom from the spell of his palpable evil, but not immediately. He muses on his close escape from being buried with Kurtz:

> I am of course aware that next day the pilgrims buried something in a muddy hole. And then they very nearly buried me. However, as you see, I did not join Kurtz there and then. (Conrad, 1988, p. 69)

Marlow survives to complete his confession and rejoin the other pilgrims of the "communion of saints" in Europe. In this sin-tainted world, where the ultimate outcome of the struggle with evil remains in doubt until the last moment of life, this communion may be called, with equal accuracy, a "communion of sinners." The resolution to return scarcely resolves the question of Marlow's destiny; his struggle for salvation must continue in a world still marred with sin. He will rejoin European society, safely returning with the boat and a portion of Kurtz's ivory. Back home, Marlow remains weakened through malaria, the external sign of moral sickness, but his case is not fatal like Kurtz's. Marlow will recover, but slowly. For a time, he keeps the lies alive through his exchanges with the company representative and Kurtz's fiancée.

While London and the Thames do not represent the impenetrable darkness of the African forest, Conrad/Marlow continually refers to the darkness and gloom of the English coastline, as though even in England the light is challenged. As Marlow begins his story he recalls the days when the Thames, like the Congo of his memories, was a land of red-haired barbarians, perfectly ripe for plunder by culturally superior Roman traders. For Conrad, light and dark, good and evil strike a precarious balance and rarely appear in absolutely pure forms. For Catholics, sin and grace similarly struggle for supremacy in the soul of the individual.

At death Kurtz's struggle is resolved. He faces "the horror"—damnation, the ultimate horror for a believer—because he has continually chosen isolation from the community, not only geographic isolation but the moral isolation of one who has created his own rules and who defies the conventions of the "enlightened" world. In the Catholic imagination, being in the communion is key to salvation. [The Protestant imagination, by contrast, finds virtue in individualism (Blake, 2000; Greeley, 1990, 1995, 2000; Tracy, 1989).] By making himself "god," Kurtz placed his own interests above those of the trading company, his nation, his fiancée, and especially the African people who served him with such misplaced devotion. Marlow must confront this tension between his fascination, even admiration, for Kurtz as the defiant individualist and his own obligations to the company, and ultimately to European culture, both of which Kurtz has betrayed. Furthermore, his suggestion, "Exterminate all the brutes," indicates quite clearly that he has not merely rejected a corrupt mercantile society for a more pristine one. He has rejected African culture as well. He chooses to remain totally alone, without roots in any society whatever. In Catholic terminology, Kurtz has deliberately excommunicated himself. He dies in this state of isolation.

The Conscience of the Vietnam War

While Conrad and his fellow Victorians might have used the evils of colonialism as a prism to examine personal responsibility in the midst of a morally ambiguous universe, Americans of the 1960s and 1970s were equally distraught by the conundrums posed by the long, bloody and seemingly unwinnable war in Vietnam. The war was as much a moral issue as a political one. Like the American public at large, religious leaders, among them many Catholics, were bitterly divided on the many issues it raised. Some, like Cardinal Francis Spellman of New York, whose office also directed all U.S. military chaplains, believed that the war was a crusade to save the world from the advance of atheistic Communism. Others, like Daniel and Phillip Berrigan and Dorothy Day, saw the campaign as an act of naked American imperialism, a moral abomination foisted upon a noble people striving for independence after years of oppression, first by the French and then by the Americans. Since it came along at the same point in history as the civil rights movement in the United States, the two issues became fused, and the racial implications of an American government's fighting an Asian war added another dimension to the debate. Some condemned the military for the extraordinary brutality of its tactics, like carpet bombing and forced relocation, and of its new high-tech ordnance, like napalm, Agent Orange, and cluster bombs. Others found fault with the American strategy of pursuing limited objectives with limited means. The war, these critics reasoned, dragged on and casualties multiplied simply because the country did not have the will nor did it supply the means to win quickly and decisively. For some, nuclear weapons seemed a reasonable means to achieve a desirable and attainable end.

John Milius's (1969) version of the script certainly reflects a pro-military, anti-pacifist viewpoint on the conflict. Based loosely on the framework of Conrad's story, Milius has the army send Captain B. L. Willard into the jungle to kill Colonel Walter Kurtz, who has spun out of control and is violating the rules of war in his pursuit of the enemy. He is winning, but not the way the Pentagon would like. Kurtz, in the Milius version, is a mediocre officer, who achieves greatness through combat, but he gradually loses his sanity because the high command will not support his tactics. He turns to drugs, rejects orders, executes suspects and pursues the war in his own way, making his own rules of engagement.

After a series of adventures on his way upriver, including fire fights and sexual liaisons, Capt. Willard grows in admiration of Kurtz, appreciates his tactics and chooses to fight with him, first against the Vietnam regulars and then against an American helicopter rescue team. When Kurtz is killed in a grotesquely violent battle, Willard assumes command and continues firing at the Americans, ". . . laughing maniacally. The others are laughing, too" (Milius, 1969, p. 131).

As writer for the *Dirty Harry* series and director for *Conan the Barbarian* (1984), John Milius has left little doubt about his belief that in the cause of righteousness, the true hero is the man who stands alone and makes his own rules in a violent world. As he started work on the script, at Coppola's request, Lyndon Johnson's war had just become Richard Nixon's war, but contrary to the expectations of many like Milius, the change in administration offered little prospect for a dramatic change in the American pursuit of victory. The outcome was still very much in doubt, and the debate within the country continued at an ever more strident level, with each side seeing the other in caricature. In an epigraph to the 1969 script, Milius recounts the anecdote of a soldier, shipping out to Vietnam, who grew impatient with a "long-haired" protester and smashed the "hippie" in the head with his helmet. When the commanding officer asked who was responsible, the unit responded as one: "I did—sir." A bystander comments: "Just think what they'll be like when they come back" (Milius, 1969). Milius seems to approve of this way of handling protesters, and uses the incident to introduce his notion that this war brings men into contact with their primitive instincts, where they can handle annoyances with dispatch. The poetic title of the script derives from a direct response to a drug culture slogan popular on some campuses: "Nirvana Now" (Cowie, 1994, p. 120).

Milius begins and ends his screenplay with scenes of unimaginable, and probably unfilmable, violence, which Coppola describes in Eleanor Coppola's documentary film *Hearts of Darkness: A Filmmaker's Apocalypse* (1991) as having a "comic book" quality. In the first scene, Kurtz and his war-painted soldiers ambush and massacre a unit of North Vietnamese regulars. Kurtz wears psychedelic sunglasses and a loincloth. One American begins to scalp the fallen enemy soldiers, while his comrades search their victims for hashish (Milius, 1969). They have clearly rejected the restraints of civilized society and have become pure warriors living according to their own internal code of morality. During his travels upriver, Willard gradually realizes that this is the only way for a soldier to live. In the final suicidal defense of the compound, Willard stands over the body of the fallen Kurtz and opens fire on the American rescue helicopters rather than accept once again the restraints of civilization.

Milius is clear that society also places unreasonable restraints on the sexual urges of the warrior, which become not only understandable, but commendable, as an expression of life in the face of death. To pass the time, the sailors on the patrol boat boast about their experiences in a massage parlor (Milius, 1969). As the troops await the arrival of the USO show, featuring Playboy bunnies, a segment that remains in the finished film, Milius comments on the crowd: "All have one thing in common—to see and if possible grab an American girl. Their need far surpasses that of the run-of-the-mill rapist, pervert or child molester" (p. 56). The army has built a moat and posted guards "to counter their need." During the suggestive and deliberately taunting dance, the audience rushes the stage and the entertainers run back to the helicopters and fly away to safety. This much appears in the film. The Milius script, however, continues the incident by having a sailor reminisce about a sergeant who shot a Vietnamese officer for confiscating his copy of the magazine containing his favorite foldout. The murderer is convicted, but Milius has the storyteller and his friends "shake their heads at the injustice of life" (p. 59).

Milius has the Playboy bunnies return later in the script in a two-part sequence that involves Willard personally. In the first part, a segment that Coppola, rewrote, shot, and then discarded altogether, the patrol boat stops at a French plantation. During an elaborate dinner, the plantation owner (Christian Marquand) vehemently repeats his intention to stay and protect his property from *any* invader, Vietnamese or American. When the dinner has ended his daughter Roxanne (Aurore Clément), a war widow, leads Willard to her bedchamber. When he awakens the next morning she tells him that while he slept soundly she ordered ammunition confiscated from the boat for the plantation (Milius, 1969). The men, who have not received such hospitality, are outraged at Willard's seemingly irresponsible conduct. In Coppola's early version, Willard sneaks back to the boat as Roxanne sleeps, kills the French soldiers guarding the boat, hides the guns and ammunition under the deck and fills the crates with sand and rocks, like a wily Odysseus outwitting a conniving Siren (Coppola, 1975).

In the second part of this episode in the Milius script, Willard soon has an opportunity to deflect the crew's anger. As warrior himself, Willard understands that sexual gratification is a normal compensation for the warrior's lot, and it is the officer's obligation to provide it for his men as well as for himself. The patrol boat comes upon the USO helicopter, now stranded for lack of fuel. Willard seizes the opportunity. After a prolonged negotiation with the emcee Willard arranges to provide sexual favors for himself and the four members of his crew: The three bunnies in exchange for two barrels of fuel. The women seem to accept their assignment as routine. Coppola retained this scene in the 1975 script, but placed it before the plantation sequence, thus eliminating the connection between Willard's receiving sexual favors and then feeling obliged to provide the same for his crew. As the Willard character matured into a more introspective character, Coppola dropped the scene altogether.

In other situations as well, women function as mere incidentals of war, to be used like any other commodity. In the famous helicopter attack on the village, the Milius screenplay contains a montage of women manning machine guns and grenade launchers as they await the attack from Colonel Kharnage, who has the equally gory name Kilgore, in the 1975 Coppola script and in the film, as played by Robert Duvall. In the Milius screenplay and in the early Coppola version, the women are merely combatants like everyone else. They must be destroyed without pity. In the scenes he added to Kilgore's raid, Coppola shows the ambiguity of their role; at first their frantic attempts to shepherd terrified children to safety before the attack points to their traditional role as innocent victims of war. The montage underscores Kilgore's, and America's, indiscriminate savagery in the war. This would not have been a consideration in the earlier versions. As the battle winds down in the film, a lone woman tosses a grenade into a medivac helicopter. Milius is partially right after all. This particular woman is a combatant, and Kilgore kills her without hesitation, remorse or reference to gender.

In the Milius screenplay, women do not exist as persons as much as objects in a totally male world. Reading through the Kurtz's dossier, Willard finds a letter from Kurtz's wife asking where her husband is, but Kurtz never refers to her. Later, Kurtz shows Willard his "concubine pit" where his women leave only to be buried (Milius, 1969, p. 112). Lieutenant Colby, an operative who has preceded Willard into the jungle and joined forces with Kurtz (and who all but disappears in the Coppola version) has written to his wife: "Sell the house. Sell the car. Sell the kids. Find someone else. Forget it. I'm never coming back. Forget it" (p. 90). To become a pure warrior one must sever all familial ties. Willard fits the pattern. He has no one. Like the others, Willard finds meaning in his life not through family but through combat. He is ripe for following Kurtz in the way of the jungle.

The film builds to a climax in the meeting between Willard and Kurtz. For Coppola the key to Willard's development is his meeting with Kurtz; for Milius it is his meeting with combat. In the Milius script the confrontation between the two men is almost perfunctory; it's the battle that measures the men. When the patrol boat lands at the compound, Kurtz identifies Willard as an assassin, sees through his transparent cover story, and has the crew thrown into a dungeon. He takes Willard on a tour of the compound, all the while showing his contempt for conventional morality. He shows Willard his fortifications and his huge stash of drugs, ". . . enough there to buy four divisions" (p. 110). Kurtz orders a dead prisoner to be fed to the old people. Kurtz is allowing the other prisoners to starve, and Willard makes the obvious comment: "This is barbaric—evil—I have never seen such evil" (p. 111). Kurtz and the soldiers under his command take hashish, acid, and speed as they wait for the attack, first from American bombs and then from the Viet Cong. The whole episode in the camp becomes a drug-heightened hallucination.

Willard's men are brought from the dungeon to join the fighting. As the battle begins, Kurtz exhorts his troops: "We are chosen to be the warriors of heaven—in this twilight of the Gods—the Gotterdammerung. This is the Apocalypse—Now!" (Milius, 1969, p. 121). Milius spells out the violent action of the battle in gruesome (comic book) detail. When Kurtz is killed, Willard and the survivors attempt to drive off both the enemy and the rescue helicopters and maintain their status as warriors living beyond the constraints of society. The outcome of the battle hangs in the balance; in the end Willard has become just as crazed as Kurtz.

Coppola's Inward Turn

By the time Francis Coppola turned his attention to the screenplay and began preproduction planning, the Vietnam War had been lost and the long, fitful process of healing had begun. The various debates about waging the war were receding from the national consciousness, and Americans of every political stripe began to feel relief that the war was over. In this atmosphere Coppola gradually began to switch the emphasis back to Conrad's story of one man's journey of self-discovery and possible redemption.

By December 1975 Coppola began this process with his own rewrite of the Milius script. He retains the opening battle sequence, which introduces Kurtz and his savage warriors, but from there the action turns to a yacht, where Willard serves as a security guard during a cocktail party. Some years after his tour of duty, Willard begins to tell his story, as a form of confession, just as Charlie Marlow had. From this point on, the story is Willard's, told from his point of view.

With his desire to change the emphasis from action to reflection, it made perfect sense for Coppola to recast Willard after only a week of shooting. Harvey Keitel, the original Willard, radiates a sense of edgy violence that fit perfectly with the original Milius conception of the character. Landing Martin Sheen, boyish looking but tough, reserved and reflective, was a stroke of genius, or good luck. The new Willard drank heavily in Saigon, but not in the jungle. He did not take drugs with the sailors on the patrol boat. He did not seize opportunities for sexual encounters, nor did he try to provide them for his men. His name changed from Booger Lewis Willard (Booger is a big name in Arkansas), to Benjamin, the youngest son of Jacob, from whom descended the nation of Israel. The character is no longer a hard-living, quick-shooting good ol' boy. In the 1975 Coppola script, he still smokes marijuana with the crew, but he cannot drink anything stronger than beer because of a history of hepatitis (Coppola, 1975). Incidentally, Captain Kharnage in the Milius script wore a Confederate cavalry hat. By 1975, Coppola marked his eccentricity with an LA Dodgers baseball cap; by the time Robert Duvall appeared as Captain Kilgore, the hat had become a blue U. S. Cavalry Stetson, still a mark of eccentricity, but also a mark of a military professional rather than a California surfer. The surfing scenes were cut drastically in the final version.

Both the opening battle sequence and the scene on the yacht were also cut, and the film began with the scene of Willard alone and drunk in a Saigon hotel room, half dreaming, half hallucinating about jungle combat. His voice-over narrative and commentary leave little doubt that this will be Willard's story, told from his perspective, not to an imagined audience, like the people on Conrad's ship or on Coppola's yacht, but directly to the audience (Watson, 1980). The device creates a disturbing intimacy during the long, painful voyage of self-revelation.

Willard reveals quite a bit about himself in his solitary reflection in the hotel. He has returned to Vietnam for a second tour after a short visit home, where he finds that after his war experience he can no longer communicate with his wife. They divorce. In addition, he no longer feels at home in his own country and longs to return to the jungle; he has served as an assassin on several occasions in the past. Willard, like Kurtz, has no community, and unlike Marlow, he has a past that includes murder. He is closed in on himself, away from an army base, looking out on the world through the slats of a venetian blind. He admires himself in the mirror, but as he continues gazing at himself, he smashes the glass as though he cannot bear what he sees. He cuts his hand and collapses on the bed.

Willard's solitude deepens as the script matures. In the Milius version, Willard is sunning himself on a beach crowded with Marines taking a break from combat when he is summoned to headquarters. In his early script Coppola has him meet the agents in a Saigon bar, but in the film the two officers find him drunk, naked and alone in his hotel room. They give him his orders and then drag him into a shower. As the cold water strikes him he groans horribly, beginning his arduous path to redemption through the blood of his cut hand and the water of the shower, two images traditionally connected with redemption: Christ's blood shed during the crucifixion and the waters of baptism. Conrad, likewise, fuses these images during one of Marlow's great moments of self-discovery. His helmsman has been struck by a spear, and as Marlow tries to help him, the man's blood pours over Marlow's shoes (Conrad, 1988). In a panic, he throws the shoes overboard. In the early script, Coppola added this scene to the Milius script, but later has Willard simply remove his boots and try to wipe away the blood.

The process of purification will not be easy for Willard, even with the sacramental help of blood and water. In voice-over he muses: "I wanted a mission and for my sins they gave me one." The sentence sets the theme of atonement, but the words are ambiguous. To paraphrase, it can mean either: They gave me a mission to punish me because of the sins I have committed (the obvious meaning); or they gave me a mission to heal me of the effects of the sins I have committed. The line does not appear in the Milius script at all, since his Willard, as a warrior, has little interest in questions of morality. As Willard continues his journey into the self through his examination of conscience and confession, and as its meaning evolves from Milius's concept to Coppola's, the second meaning becomes more important.

Willard will gradually discover the sinfulness within and root it out, like lancing a boil, so that he can be saved.

After smashing the mirror to indicate the terror he finds in looking at himself, Willard receives his mission at command headquarters, where he denies three times that he had any involvement with assassination. The triple denial, added to the Milius dialogue, goes beyond the realistic defense of secrecy; it emphasizes Willard's inability to admit the truth about himself. During lunch the officers play a tape of Kurtz, who describes his dream of a snail crawling down the edge of a straight razor. The snail can fall either way, or cut itself in half by remaining on the edge. Kurtz has fallen onto the side of evil; Willard may go either way. As General Corman (G. D. Spradlin) explains:

> There is a conflict in every human heart between the rational and the irrational, between good and evil, and good does not always triumph. Sometimes the dark side overcomes what Lincoln called the better angels of our nature. (Milius, 1969, p. 80)

As they listen to Kurtz's voice, the camera focuses on a close up of an untrimmed shrimp on a platter with its eye staring out at Willard. The general has told Willard that if he can face these snail-like creatures, he will have no further need to prove his bravery.

Among the crimes they impute to Kurtz during their conversation at lunch is the assassination of four Vietnamese suspected of being double agents; Willard has already murdered at least six. Willard shows an almost prophetic sense of the communality in evil between himself and Kurtz. As they were entering the General's bungalow Willard's voice-over warns us: "There is no way of telling his [Kurtz's] story without telling mine. And if his story is a confession then so is mine."

Willard's sense of communal guilt extends beyond Kurtz. Like Conrad's Marlow, who discovers that he participates in the horrors of colonialism, Willard shares all the madness of the war simply by being an American and being there, a proposition that Milius could never have accepted. Martin Sheen's Willard remains oddly passive as he observes the effects of the war. Assuming Willard's point of view, Coppola views the drug usage, the near riot during the *Playboy* show, and especially the violence of combat with a clinical, nonjudgmental eye, all the while very much aware that this war, with its remote jungle setting and premature confrontation with death, is pushing these soldiers further into a state of primitive barbarism. Is it possible for Willard to remain untouched by all of this?

During two combat sequences, Willard coolly observes the cowboy tactics of Lt. Col. Kilgore with a mixture of horror and admiration. War has become a game for Kilgore. He struts through the battlefield, in his bizarre costume, marking the bodies of the fallen with playing cards engraved with the emblem of the First Cavalry, but he can be easily distracted by the discovery that a famous surfer has arrived. The war has become a game for the American people as well. Willard is stunned to find a camera crew, led by Coppola himself, filming the battle. Coppola, the actor, tells him not to look at the camera but to pretend he's fighting. On the second day, Kilgore leads a helicopter attack accompanied by Wagner's *Ride of the Valkyries*. Again, in the midst of unspeakable violence, Kilgore is distracted by the thought of surfing while the battle continues. For his part Willard appears never to have fired a shot, nor does he show any interest in surfing. In the Milius script and in Coppola's 1975 version, Willard and his crew steal Kilgore's best surfboard to show his gradual loss of moral sense, but in the final version, they simply observe Kilgore with horror and amazement and leave without another mention of surfing (Coppola, 1975).

Any hope, however, that Willard might have of keeping himself aloof from the degradation that he witnesses vanishes with one definitive gesture. In a scene added to the film during shooting, the patrol boat stops a sampan to search for weapons. A girl's sudden movement provokes a rain of automatic weapons fire from the patrol boat. Everyone aboard the sampan is dead except the girl, who is severely wounded. Rather than allow the crew to take her to a field hospital, Willard coolly murders her with a single shot from his side arm. Coppola adds a particularly sentimental touch to underline the barbarity of the act. The crew discovers that the sampan carries only food, and the girl moved to protect a small puppy, which the sailors cradle in their arms as they weep at realization of their senseless atrocity. In that single scene, Coppola shows that the more deeply Willard recedes into the darkness of the jungle, the more he absorbs primitive evil, just as Kurtz had. In this environment, they are all sinners: Willard, Kurtz, the crew, the army, the country.

By murdering the girl, Willard reveals his own capacity for evil. His is a single, unpremeditated act, but in the meeting with Kurtz, he sees the horrifying effects of systematic evil embraced as a way of life. He is fascinated, but also revolted at what he sees. The compound is decorated with heads and other decaying body parts, but the references to cannibalism and the concubine pit have been removed. The photojournalist (Dennis Hopper), a crazed Russian in Conrad and an Australian deserter in the early Coppola, tells Willard: "You don't talk to Colonel Kurtz. You listen to him" (Coppola, 1975, p. 100). Listen he does. And he learns. Kurtz (Marlon Brando) delivers a chilling monologue. He has placed himself above all the petty morality of the outside world. He derides Willard as a mere "errand boy sent by grocery clerks." With more admiration than revulsion, he tells of the guerrillas who amputated the arms of children inoculated by American medics; they are not hindered by the moral considerations of others. With dedicated, amoral warriors like that, Kurtz claims he could win the war in months. He tells Willard that he has the right to kill him but not to judge him.

With this statement Kurtz seems to invite death. His reading of T. S. Eliot's "The Hollow Men" along with the shot of James Frazer's *The Golden Bough* suggest that Kurtz realizes that it is time for him to die. According to Frazer, some primitive peoples believe that a young pretender must kill their king at the first sign of his decline so that his magical powers might pass to his murderer and successor to the throne (Tessitore, 1979). Kurtz is in decline, but he could surely have had Willard killed at any time. In fact, after their conversation he has him confined to a tiger cage. The photojournalist gives Willard water and a cigarette and rants on in a near frenzy about alternatives: "You either love someone or you hate them." Willard makes his decision when Kurtz tosses the severed head of Chief (Frederic Forest) into the tiny cell with Willard. He has seen pure evil in Kurtz and must destroy it. With this decision he goes forward with the assassination, but since Coppola gives no indication of how he gets out, it is possible to understand the tiger cage in metaphorical terms. Willard is bound by his own hesitation in judging good and evil, but when he finally recognizes pure evil, as embodied in Kurtz, he is freed from his own limitations and can proceed with the work. The decapitation of Chef provides a proleptic reference to the beheading of the carabao that will signify Willard's ultimate triumph.

While Conrad has Marlow reach his redemption by recognizing the evil in Kurtz and leaving him buried in a mud hole, Coppola has Willard take a far more active role than Marlow in working out his salvation. The complex visual imagery reveals much of the progress of Willard's journey. In keeping with the Catholic sacramental sense of physical object—material realities vividly presented often bear a spiritual import—Coppola devises an association of visual images to provide the same kind of philosophic or religious reflection that Conrad did with Marlow's lengthy monologues.

In the film, Willard's liberation from Kurtz and thus from his own "dark side," to use General Corman's phrase, comes in the climactic sequence when Willard finally murders Kurtz. The scene is intercut with the ritual slaughter of a carabao, or water buffalo (French, 1998). The imagery of cattle and slaughter winds through the entire film. During the general's lunch with Willard, the photograph of Kurtz appears prominently in the background as a platter of roast beef is passed around the table (Grieff, 1992). Thus the images of meat and Kurtz are fused from the beginning, and, significantly, the folder with Kurtz's picture falls to the floor as they discuss plans "to terminate with extreme prejudice."

The image reappears with unambiguously religious overtones during the first of Colonel Kilgore's battle scenes. While the fighting continues, with Coppola's camera crew recording the action for American television audiences and Kilgore strutting among the dead dropping First Cavalry playing cards on the bodies, the camera fixes on the improbable scene of a Catholic chaplain in the final stages of offering a Mass for soldiers. They are all standing around the altar, where they would be likely targets for enemy fire. As they recite the Lord's Prayer, which comes near the end of the liturgy, a helicopter lifts a carabao over the altar.

This baffling surrealistic touch rarely receives mention, but it states the theme of redemption that Coppola and Conrad each develop in his own terms. French (1998), for example, avoids interpreting the scene altogether when he writes: "This aerial cow sequence demonstrates the strength of the modern Huey helicopter" (pp. 25–26). He includes no reference to the religious service in the foreground. For those familiar with the Catholic tradition, the "Holy Sacrifice of the Mass," as Catholics formally call it, is the actual reliving of the sacrifice of Christ on the cross in atonement for the sins of the world. He takes sin upon himself, and allows himself to be immolated like a sacrificial animal; and by his death, he frees the world from the bondage of sin. In his death, he destroys sin. In their iconography, Catholics stress the horrible disfigurement caused by the presence of sin with their finely detailed images of Christ in his death agony on a crucifix, while Protestants tend to favor the more abstract, plain cross without an affixed "corpus" or body of Christ. The soldiers verbalize the message with their prayer: "Forgive us our trespasses"; "deliver us from evil." The Lord's Prayer leads to a sharing of the Eucharist, in which Catholics find solidarity with the entire communion of saints.

At the climax of the film, the slaughter of the carabao, in tandem with the murder of Kurtz, finally accomplishes the freedom from the evil that threatened to overwhelm Willard. The image of the carabao thus relates both to the death of Kurtz and to the death of Christ. Through this sacrifice Willard finds redemption. At the same time it should be clear that Coppola intended neither Willard nor Kurtz nor the sacrificed animal to be understood as a "Christ symbol." He is too subtle an artist to offer simplistic one-to-one allegories. He and Conrad are both grappling with the dynamics of salvation. To achieve salvation, one must identify evil in the world and in the self (the examination of conscience) and then take the means (confession and atonement) to destroy it.

In this light the ending that Coppola agonized over for several years, through focus groups and pressure from the studio to finish the project, appears not as the disappointment that Coppola believed it to be but as the absolutely perfect ending that the story demanded as it developed from Conrad. To allow Willard to assume the role of Kurtz after the execution, or to have him call in the air strike to destroy the village and himself, two endings Coppola considered, would have undercut the theme of redemption that he appropriated from Conrad as he reworked the Milius script.

For Conrad, it was important for Marlow to leave the remains of Kurtz in the darkness and return to Europe with the knowledge that Kurtz can no longer touch him. Coppola follows the same pattern, but allows Willard to take more vigorous action by killing Kurtz with a sword much like the one used to sacrifice the carabao. Willard leaves the body and picks up Kurtz's typescript, on which he had scrawled: "Drop the bomb. Exterminate them all." It is the record of Kurtz's evil unmasked, the confession Kurtz did not live to make, but which Willard has not appropriated as his own.

Willard, however, does not allow himself to become another Kurtz. He has conquered Kurtz and what he represents. Once he has returned to the boat, he switches off the radio and severs the connection with the dispatcher who is asking for coordinates in order to call in a "purgative" air strike to destroy the compound and Willard. Willard will not try to "purge" the heart of darkness in himself by suicidal fire. He chooses to live. To redeem himself, Willard can neither surrender to evil nor can he destroy it. Nor can he destroy himself. He must return home, where he will continue to live in a sin-stained world with his message of salvation, just like Charlie Marlow.

Coppola himself claims to have wanted to leave Willard's redemption in doubt. In an interview he claimed that the present ending is a "lie" forced on him by test audiences (Marcus, 1979). Initially, he wanted to end with Willard standing in the doorway after the murder, while Kurtz's voice-over repeated: "The horror! The horror!" Coppola felt that the true horror that Willard faced was the decision, whether to become Kurtz or to leave. That moment of decision recalls Kurtz's dream of the snail crawling on the razor. The present ending offers a resolution for Willard. By beginning the journey back to civilization, to a communion, Willard embraces Christian redemption, much as Conrad's Charlie Marlow had.

The closure is complete. Willard first appears on screen with his face in close-up, upside down at the left of the screen. It slowly turns 90 degrees under the rotating blades of the ceiling fan. The dizzying instability suggests a state of moral vertigo. When Willard last appears on the screen, he is again in close-up at the left of the screen, but this time it is straight up, and gradually blends in split screen with a partially submerged stone Buddha. The vertigo has been resolved into the timeless truth of good and evil. The boat in the foreground begins its journey back down river, bathed by cleansing, baptismal waters.

Milius, Coppola, Herr and the critics who offered initial reactions to *Apocalypse Now* were all, to a greater or lesser extent, overshadowed by the moral context of the Vietnam War, just as Conrad and his critics were preoccupied with questions of colonialism. As the years pass, the once timely political issues recede and the timeless interior struggles of Willard and Marlow figure more prominently in our appreciation of the two works of art. These internal conflicts have been shaped from a moral tradition with a decidedly religious background, and in the case of both Joseph Conrad and Francis Coppola, a decidedly Catholic imagination.

REFERENCES

Blake, R. A. (2000). *Afterimage: The Indelible Catholic Imagination of Six American Filmmaker*s. Chicago, IL: Loyola Press.

Catholic Church. (1994). *Catechism of the Catholic Church.* (St. Paul Books and Media, Trans.). Vatican City: Libreria Editrice Vaticana.

Conrad, J. (1988). *Heart of Darkness*, Robert Kimbrough (Ed.). New York: Norton.

Coppola, F. F. (1975, December 3). *Apocalypse Now.*

Cowie, P. (1994). *Coppola, a Biography.* New York, NY: DaCapo.

French, K. (1998). *Karl French on Apocalypse Now.* New York, NY: Bloomsbury.

Greeley, A. M. (1990). *The Catholic Myth: The Behavior and Beliefs of American Catholics.* New York, NY: Scribners.

Greeley, A. M. (1995). *Religion as Poetry.* New Brunswick, NJ: Transaction Publishers.

Greeley, A. M. (2000). *The Catholic Imagination.* Berkley, CA: University of California Press.

Grieff, L. K. (1992). "Soldier, sailor, surfer, chef: Conrad's ethics and the margins of *Apocalypse Now.*" *Literature Film Quarterly, 20* (3), 92.

Guerard, A. J. (1965). *Conrad the Novelist.* Cambridge, MA: Harvard University Press.

Kimbrough, R. (Ed.). (1988). *Heart of Darkness.* New York, NY: Norton.

Lester, J. (1988). *Conrad and Religion.* New York, NY: St. Martin's.

Lordeaux, L. (1990). *Italian and Irish Filmmakers in America.* Philadelphia, PA: Temple University Press.

Marcus, G. (1979, November 1). Journey up the river: An interview with Francis Coppola. *Rolling Stone*, pp. 56–57.

McBrien, R. (1980). *Catholicism* (Vols. 1–2). Minneapolis, MN: Winston Press.

Milius, J. (1969, December 5). *Apocalypse Now.* First draft.

Tessitore, J. (1979, October 21). "The literary roots of *Apocalypse Now.*" *The New York Times*, p. D21.

Tracy, D. (1989). *The Analogical Imagination: Christian Theology and the Culture of Pluralism.* New York, NY: Crossroad.

Watson, W. (1980). "Willard as narrator: A critique and an immodest proposal." *Conradiana, 13,* (1), 35–44.

Watt, I. (1979). *Conrad in the Nineteenth Century.* Berkeley, CA: University of California.

The Modern Catholic University: How Far from Eden?

Robert B. Lawton, S.J.

66 "In the Modern Catholic University: How Far from Eden?," reflects on the place of non-Catholics at a Catholic university. Would such a university, if entirely or overwhelmingly Catholic in its faculty, staff, and students, be Eden, or close to it? Viewed another way, was there a paradise in the past of most of this country's Catholic universities, a time, albeit idealized, when these institutions were "truly" Catholic, a moment from which they have moved, now somewhere on a path paralleling that of once Protestant universities that became entirely secular? In short, is there an Eden toward which Catholic universities should journey or from which they have exiled themselves?

These large questions bring with them a more particular, quite personal one. If I am a non-Catholic at a Catholic university, why am I here? Because of legal requirements (institutions cannot discriminate based on religion); by default (there simply are not enough Catholics in my discipline, professional field, or fitting my student profile); in order to advance the university's prestige (even if there are enough, the Catholics are not as qualified); or for other reasons. Certain declarations in *Ex Corde Ecclesiae: An Application to the United States* (2000) encourage such questions: "To the extent possible, the majority of the Board should be Catholics committed to the Church (p. 2.6) . . . the university president should be a Catholic (p. 3.a) . . . the university should strive to recruit and appoint Catholics as professors so that, to the extent possible, those committed to the witness of the faith will constitute a majority of the faculty" (p. 4.a). Put most starkly: If I am non-Catholic, would the university prefer, all things being equal, to have a Catholic in my place?

Various approaches to this topic suggest themselves: a philosophical one, for example, examining the nature of a university; a theological one, looking at the nature of the Church; or an historical one, reflecting on the histories of religiously oriented institutions. I would like to make a more personal analysis, contemplating my own lived experience of Catholic universities.

The British mathematician and philosopher Alfred North Whitehead (1929) has written:

> The true method of discovery is like the flight of an airplane. It starts from the ground of particular observation; it makes a flight in the thin air of imaginative generalization; and it again lands for renewed observation rendered acute by rational interpretation. (1978, p. 5)

I will begin with some particular observations, then attempt to generalize. I will conclude with renewed observations, I trust "rendered acute by rational interpretation" (Whitehead, 1978, p. 5).

I was the Dean of Georgetown College at Georgetown University for a decade (1989–1999). For much of that time, I interviewed the finalists for every faculty position. A person's religion never played any role in his or her being hired or not, not once. "Fit" with the university's mission and culture, yes, but never religion. Why?

Toward the end of his *The History of England in the Eighteenth Century*, T.B. Macaulay (1980) discusses an 1828 act of Parliament requiring a person taking office ". . . to make a declaration on the true faith of a Christian" (p. 260). He observes:

> The points of difference between Christianity and Judaism have very much to do with a man's fitness to be a bishop or a rabbi. But they have no more to do with his fitness to be a magistrate, legislator, or a minister of finance, than with his fitness to be a cobbler. Nobody has ever thought of compelling cobblers to make any declaration on the true faith of a Christian. Any man would rather have his shoes mended by a heretical cobbler than by a person who has subscribed to all the thirty-nine articles but had never handled an awl. Men act thus, not because they are indifferent to religion, but because they do not see what religion has to do with the mending of their shoes. (Macaulay, 1980, p. 260)

A person's religion, in nearly every case, has nothing to do, in any simple way, with his or her qualifications to teach or to research a discipline; a baptismal certificate is not an additional degree. The notable exception, of course, is theology, and in such hires a number of considerations are brought explicitly to bear; even here a person's religion is rarely determinative. A person's abilities to explore the natural world and the world of culture, to make knowledge, to nourish wisdom, to educate the young, to be a good colleague, to fit into and contribute to an institution's ethos are the relevant factors in faculty hires, with analogous qualifications for staff and administrators.

Granted that this is true in each individual case—what about the collective? No matter what the qualifications for any given position, faculty, staff, or administrative, are not a significant number of Catholics necessary at an institution to preserve and enhance its Catholic character? The argument here seems strong, even obvious. It also seems, at least to me, merely seductive. My own experience at Georgetown was that a significant number of those who worked to strengthen the university's Catholic identity were not Catholic. An even larger number contributed to those aspects of the university and its life that its Catholicity fostered and held dear.

Why? Why should non-Catholics be interested in promoting a university's Catholic character? Quite simply, a Catholic university can be seen as creating a culture and fostering values that a person can cherish without, at the same time, accepting faith elements that undergird or motivate that culture and its values. It is, in the end, not surprising, that non-Catholics could be passionately committed to a university that takes religious and ethical questions seriously, that promotes community service, and that is interested in spirituality broadly defined.

Looked at collectively, there is an even deeper reason for a Catholic university to value the non-Catholics in its midst. Those of us who are Catholic benefit enormously from the presence of people whose ways of viewing God and the world are far different from our own. Such people question our clichés, shake our categories, stretch our imaginations, and touch our hearts. God is far too big, God's world far too intricately textured, to be exhausted by the insights of any one tradition, religious or intellectual, or even by the sum of all traditions. Macaulay once observed that the Jesuits ". . . appear to have discovered the precise point to which intellectual culture can be carried without risk of intellectual emancipation" (Macaulay, 1980, p. 260). The presence of non-Catholics makes intellectual emancipation likelier and, with it, deeper soundings of reality's richness—and, for the Catholic, greater appreciation of God's awesome majesty.

With all this as a background, let me briefly generalize about the marks of a Catholic university. The Catholic Church contributes most significantly to the life of a university by giving the university a goal beyond itself, a context for all it does. For all its bungling, complexity, and sinfulness, the Church got into and remains in colleges and universities because it believes that education touches lives, that it enables people to live more deeply and to dream large, to develop their talents and deploy them at the world's service. This mission corresponds to a hope that many people, Catholic or not, have for their lives, the hope that we can help at least a few people to grow and be more fully themselves. A Catholic university always sees itself in light of this larger vision.

A Catholic university expands and deepens the questions normally asked at a university. Considerations of ultimate meaning and value, of the existence of God, of what is right and ethical, feel at home on a Catholic campus. Cynicism, indifference, and derision do not push them out. Catholic universities should have strong theology departments and ethics programs, and campus ministry should be vibrant. Ideally, a Catholic university should have faculty positions and programs dedicated to making apparent the riches of the Catholic intellectual tradition, (e.g., Church history, Catholic social teaching). It should also house Catholic intellectuals interested in dialogue with the larger world. The university's Catholic character should be prominent in its mission statement and admissions material and a driving force in its strategic planning.

Who is responsible for maintaining and enhancing the Catholic character of the university over time? Until recently, the reply seemed obvious: the sponsoring religious community or communities. Demographic trends now preclude so easy an answer. Faculty/staff groups, concerned about the university's religious character can, of course, do wonderful things to care for that character, but such groups depend too much on a few people and their initiative, availability, and other interests over time. Ultimate responsibility for a university's character, and not simply for its financial strength, rests with the Board of Trustees. The Board owns the university and cares for it over time. It seems to me that a university's Catholicity is ultimately in Board hands. How a Board chooses to carry out this charge will differ according to place and time. Boards, of course, must be helped to recognize and exercise this responsibility, and Board members must be chosen in light of it.

Among the items that a Board needs to nourish are the marks listed in the "generalization" above: theology and ethics; campus ministry; and faculty positions bringing to bear the Church's intellectual tradition and positions for Catholic intellectuals; the mission statement; admissions material, and strategic planning. There is one other area that bears watching too. With a religiously diverse faculty, staff, and student body, it is understandable that a Catholic university's rhetoric could tend to become merely humanistic, increasingly emptied of religious terms, traditions, and symbols. That would be inappropriate. Part of a university's being "Catholic" is that it continues to speak about itself in faith-infused language.

In hiring, a Catholic university understandably looks for a "fit" with its mission. Is there any category of persons who would not fit? Anyone who believes, even if for good reasons, that religion is inimical to the intellectual life and that it retards people's full development of themselves would not be appropriate as a faculty, staff, or Board member at a Catholic university. Such persons could be understandably committed to secularizing the institution over time.

The modern Catholic university: How far from Eden? What would such an Eden be like? How would a university filled exclusively with talented, creative, intelligent, committed Catholics function? What significant contributions would it make to the education of the young, the increase of knowledge, the fostering of wisdom? We can only guess or dream. What was the original Eden like? In Catholic tradition it is common to speak of the sin of Adam and Eve that led to the expulsion from Eden as a "happy fault," because it led to God's coming among us in Christ. However far we are from Eden, the experience of the modern Catholic university is that God dwells more fully among us precisely because of the presence of non-Catholics on the faculty and staff.

REFERENCES

Catholic Church (2000). *Ex Corde Ecclesiae: An Application to the United States*. Washington, D.C.: United States Catholic Conference.

Macaulay, T. B. (1980). *The History of England in the Eighteenth Century.*
      London: The Folio Society.

Whitehead, A. N. (1978, c1929). *Process and Reality: An Essay in
      Cosmology.* New York: Free Press.

PART II

Reflections on the Life Force of the
Catholic Tradition

Imagining Justice: Is Law Like Love?

Scott Wood

Robert Bellah urges the use of analogical imagination to transmit essential values in the university; to employ metanarratives which engage the student's imaginative rather than critical faculties. This means teaching which, in contrast to dialogical critiques, aims to transmit a positive vision of human life and its possibilities:

> What the students need above all is substance, is metanarratives, that will give them some sense of who they are and what kind of world they live in. Only that would counter the incoherence that surrounds them and give them a context in which the skills of critical thinking would make sense. (Bellah, 2003, p. 44)

In his own experience, Bellah finds that Christian metanarratives provide the analogies, the similarities in the relationships between and among God, self, society, and world. In his most provocative statement, Bellah asserts that, in a Catholic university, the most important thing is that it is a worshipping community with the Mass and the Eucharist at the heart of common life: "It is there that the analogical imagination takes over our consciousness and makes all things real" (Bellah, 2003, p. 46). But he wisely adds that linking that experience to the individual lives of students, a diverse group including those of other religious traditions and nonbelievers, is a matter of persuasion, a labor of love.

Bellah cites a book by Hans Joas (2000), *The Genesis of Values*, to make this ultimate point. He explains that Joas devotes his final chapter to the issue of reconciling the right and the good:

> The right necessarily always involves constraint; laws must be enforced. But we are drawn to the good by love. Joas (2000) quotes Goethe as saying, "One knows nothing save what one loves, and the deeper and more complete that knowledge, the stronger and livelier must be one's love" (Bellah, 2003, p. 47)

So, for Bellah, the analogical imagination arises from love, primarily, the love and knowledge of God expressed in prayer and worship, but also the love of "all the forms of good that overflow from God." In a university, these forms take the shape of those multiple disciplines and fields of study represented by the numerous schools and departments.

As a law professor within a Catholic university, I find Bellah's thesis particularly challenging. In my experience, the contemporary study of law is dominated by the demands of the market, both the legal job market and the larger capital market which most lawyers serve. Bellah's quote from Ann Swidler strikes a chord:

> Many come to think of their education in purely instrumental terms, just like their work lives—an accumulation of credits toward a degree that will help them in the labor market. The idea that the college years allow time for the development of deeper understanding of history, cultures, and societies outside one's own, a deepened appreciation of one's own history and traditions, and reflection on the purpose and meaning of life in society—for appropriation of the enormous cultural endowment that is our birthright, won through generations of those who came before us— this conception of education is all but lost. (Bellah, 2003, p. 43)

And since law school is a step or two removed from the college years, I am tempted to just say "lost." However, before drawing that sad conclusion, I would like to test Bellah's thesis.

Imagining Justice

During the past several years, I have taught a course entitled "Law and Literature." The list of readings includes Greek tragedies and Shakespeare plays, as well as contemporary works. Motivated by Bellah's argument, I gave fresh thought to the analogical meanings of two of the plays and their metanarratives about justice. The following is a modest effort to trace out one linking analogy.

Among the course readings is a poem by W. H. Auden (1991) with the unlikely title "Law Like Love." In the poem, the speaker begins with a litany of familiar and amusing metaphors, images of what "the law is:" "Law, says the gardener is the sun . . . Law, says the priest with a priestly look . . . is my pulpit and my steeple . . . Law, says the Judge as he looks down his nose, speaking clearly and most severely . . . Law is the law. . . ." But then the whimsical flow takes a turn as Auden forsakes the list of metaphors and ends with a simile:

> Unlike so many men
> I cannot say law *is* again,
> No more than they can we suppress
> The universal wish to guess
> Or slip out of our own position
> Into an unconcerned condition.
> Although I can at least confine
> Your vanity and mine
> To stating timidly
> A timid similarity,
> We shall boast anyway:
> Like love I say.
>
> Like love we don't know where or Why
> Like love we can't compel or fly
> Like love we often weep,
> Like love we seldom keep. (Auden, 1991, p. 262)

"Law Like Love" provides an analogy and an introduction to the following discussion of *The Eumenides* and *Measure for Measure*, a discussion which tests both Bellah's metanarrative theory and Auden's simile. Can these imaginative artifacts of legal process be read analogically to produce metanarratives? And do any such meta-narratives show that law is like love in ways which make sense, even to those inclined to regard the law in purely instrumental terms?

Greek Tragedy: *The Eumenides*

Aeschylus' production of his justly famous trilogy, *The Oresteia*, (458 BCE) depicts "the first trial of bloodshed," the birth of the jury trial (Aeschylus, 1977). The trial of Orestes for the calculated murder of his mother, Clytemnestra, Queen of Argos, confronted the Athenian audience with justice issues which were both primordial and immediate. This audience knew well the legend of the House of Atreus, the infamous family which had been trapped in murderous cycles of vengeance and intergenerational bloodshed. They knew about the horrors which occurred during the Trojan War. They also knew that their Court, the Aeropagus, had been recently subjected to radical democratic reforms. The stage was set for an exploration of the Athenians' deepest concerns about the law.

The legendary background story itself evoked pity and fear. Agamemnon, King of Argos and head of the House of Atreus, has acceded to his brother Menelaus's plea to gather the Greek warriors and sail to Troy to take back his kidnapped wife, Helen. On the outbound voyage, the gods, for inscrutable reasons, becalm the fleet and, after many days, the Greek army faces mass starvation. Agamemnon's priest propitiates the gods who, in answer to his prayers, inform the priest that they require the ritual sacrifice of Agamemnon's youngest daughter, Iphigenia. After an agonizing struggle of conscience, Agamemnon kills his daughter to save the fleet. Accordingly, the gods blow the fleet to Troy where, after 10 years of siege and battle, the Greeks achieve glorious victory. It is this moment which begins Aeschylus's trilogy: The signal fires announcing the Greek triumph light up the predawn skies over Argos.

In Argos, the horror of Iphigenia's sacrifice has lived on in the vengeful heart of her mother, Agamemnon's Queen, Clytemnestra. Moreover, during Agamemnon's long absence, she has taken up with his cousin, Aegisthus who, for deep-rooted family reasons, also hates Agamemnon. They have planned retribution.

In this first play, *Agamemnon*, Clytemnestra greets the conquering hero and Cassandra, his Trojan concubine. She invites the King to walk into the palace on sacred tapestries, which the proud Agamemnon does, despite knowing that his act is sacrilegious. Once the King and Queen are off-stage behind the doors of the palace, Cassandra, a prophetess, foretells Agamemnon's death, and her own. She then enters the palace where Clytemnestra has lured Agamemnon into a bath. When he emerges, the Queen wraps him in nets and, together with Aegisthus, stabs him and the hapless Cassandra. The victims' screams send horror and revulsion through the audience.

The second play, *The Libation Bearers*, is set at the palace of Argos 20 years after Agamemnon's assassination (Aeschylus, 1977). In connection with that killing, Clytemnestra sent away her son and Agamemnon's heir, the young prince Orestes. Now a man, Orestes has been ordered by the god Apollo to return to Argos, to exact retribution for his father's murder. He arrives disguised as a traveler and, by coincidence, meets his sister, Electra, at their father's grave where, she is offering memorial libations. She recognizes him and soon reveals her own vengeful heart. Together, they plot to kill their mother.

The second play ends with more screams behind the palace doors as Orestes kills both Clytemnestra and Aegisthus. But as the doors swing open to reveal this next family horror, the audience learns that Orestes, the pursuer of justice, is now the pursued. The Furies, implacable female deities, have arisen from the underworld to avenge the Queen's death; they enforce the primordial mandate that matricides pay for their crime with their own lives. The Furies bring a death sentence for Orestes. The play ends with Orestes fleeing, headed for Delphi, the shrine of Apollo.

The final play, *The Eumenides*, dramatizes the first trial in Western literature, the homicide trial of Orestes (Aeschylus, 1977). In the opening scene at Delphi, Apollo, although a god, can give the fleeing Orestes nothing more than ritual purging. He has no power over the Furies, older deities who enforce the primal law of retribution. Apollo sends Orestes to Athens where Athena reigns as the goddess of justice: the Furies are in hot pursuit.

Athena interviews the parties at her shrine. After understanding that Orestes killed Clytemnestra in obedience to Apollo's mandate and, further, learning that the Furies have equal and, indeed, more ancient prerogatives, Athena admits that the case "defeats me." Her solution is to move the venue, to found a court on the famous hill of Ares, in the shadow of the Acropolis. There she swears in 12 jurors and orders the litigants to ". . . summon your trusted witnesses and proofs, your defenders under oath to help your cause" (Aeschylus, 1977, p. 240).

The case opens with the Furies as prosecutors, stating their open and shut case: he killed his mother, therefore, he must die. The Furies claim their ancient right to execute matricides, notwithstanding the facts of the case, i.e. Clytemnestra's crime and Orestes's claim that Apollo ordered him to avenge his father's death.

Orestes's advocate is Apollo and, under his cross-examination, the Furies admit that Clytemnestra's murder of the King is irrelevant to them. The Queen did not kill blood kin, they say; in contrast, Orestes violated the blood bond in killing his mother. The Furies have a narrow legal interest:

> Leader [of the Furies]: Matricides: we drive them from
> their houses. Apollo: And what of the wife who strikes her
> husband down? Leader: That murder would not destroy
> one's flesh and blood. (Aeschylus, 1977, p. 240)

Apollo responds to this narrow claim with a stunning asser-
tion: Orestes had no blood bond with Clytemnestra because she, as
mother, was no real parent. No, only the father, "he who mounts," is
the real parent: as demonstrative evidence, Apollo points to the judge
herself, Athena, who was not born of woman. According to the myth,
she emerged in full battle armor from the forehead of Zeus. Since the
goddess-judge herself sprang from the patriarch alone, this proves that
the male is the only parent. The logic is inescapable: if Orestes was not
related to his mother by blood (Apollo says she was "just a nurse to
the seed") he stands on the same footing as Clytemnestra, whose
killing of Agamemnon also violated no blood bond. In a significant
foreshadowing, Apollo, Western literature's first lawyer, uses a legal
technicality for Orestes's defense.

Before the jurors cast their ballot stones, Athena delivers her
great founding speech warning the Athenians:

> Neither anarchy nor tyranny, my people.
> Worship the Mean, I urge you,
> Shore it up with reverence and never
> Banish terror from the gates, not outright.
> Where is the righteous man who knows no fear?
> The stronger your fear, your reverence for the just,
> The stronger your country's wall and city's safety.
> (Aeschylus, 1977, p. 262)

The jurors then cast their lots as the tension rises. Before the
votes are counted, Athena announces that, if it is up to her, she will
vote for acquittal, because "I cannot set more store by the woman's
death—she killed her husband, guardian of their house" (Aeschylus,
1977, p. 265). And, indeed, the decision does fall to Athena, because
the jury is deadlocked, six votes each way. Since she cannot say that
Clytemnestra's death was worse than Agamemnon's, the Furies have
not carried their burden of proof. Further, under Athena's "Rule of
Mercy," a hung jury ends Orestes's trial; she sets him free to return to
Argos where he will rule, as Athens's friend.

But the dispute between the Furies and Apollo is not over. The Furies, raging at the defeat of the old law, threaten to destroy Athens. Suddenly, Athena's court is itself on trial, and she must make a case for this novel justice system. Significantly, Athena relies on persuasion, not force, to combat the Furies' threats. Although she slyly notes that she alone among the gods knows where Zeus keeps his fatal thunderbolt, she says she will not use violence. Instead, she pleads, "Let me persuade you." She points out rightly that the Furies did not lose; the jurors were deadlocked. Further, she argues that they would regret the destruction of Athens because they would lose a home. Athena presses the point by offering them an honored place in Athens and great powers. They will dictate the fate of every family with jurisdiction over agriculture, animal husbandry and childbirth. No house will prosper without their blessing. Slowly, as Athena keeps arguing and coaxing, the Furies relent and accept her offer. They transform into "The Eumenides," the Kindly Ones. Athena proclaims:

> I enthrone these strong, implacable spirits here
> and root them in our soil.
> > Theirs,
> Theirs to rule the lives of men,
> It is their fated power. (Aeschylus, 1977, p. 272)

Athena then orders the older Athenian woman to escort the Kindly Ones to their honored place in caves under the rock hill of Ares, where they will preside and, quite literally, provide the underpinning for the court. The great trilogy ends with a torchlight procession as the audience follows the Eumenides and their escorts out of the theater. So ends the ". . . grand parable of human progress."

Both the trial of Orestes and the transformation of the vengeful Furies suggest important analogies for understanding justice. The trial dramatizes the confrontation between the primordial law of vengeance for victims of crime and the civic need for public due process, trial by jury. In the trial, the Furies' irrational passions conflict with Apollo's cold logic. Despite the seemingly irreconcilable conflict, however, Athena's founding speech warns that both sets of values are necessary; that the fear of retribution must be ever-present even as Athenians worship the mean, the rule of reason. Thus, given the equal status of passion and reason, we are not surprised that the jury deadlocks.

The work of justice is left to Athena and the art of persuasion. First, she releases Orestes under the rule of mercy. She does not declare him innocent; he is merely "not guilty as charged." Next, more importantly, Athena converts the Furies. "Like love [she] cannot compel," instead, she resorts to the art of rhetoric, arguing for broader interests. Since the Furies stand for fundamental maternal prerogatives, Athena offers them power over the family, the first "polis" and basis for civic life. They remain the guardians of the blood bond, but become protectors of the marriage bond, too. No family can prosper without them. And although Apollo's patriarchal institution, the Court of Ares, will administer the law under the rule of reason, it will depend on the Furies, too. The representatives of primal passions, now become kindly protectors of Athens, will underpin the logical processes of the Court. Due process must incorporate a passion for justice. In the end, the whole is greater than the sum of its parts.

The law of the *Oresteia* ends up looking like love. The coercive force of law, which motivates both the Furies and Apollo, yields to wiser persuasion. As in a functioning family, the marriage bonds are tied by love, as are the blood bonds which link parent to child, child to sibling. And the respect for these bonds unites families within tribes and tribes within Athens' democratic polis. The common good, law's goal, depends on love.

The metanarrative that emerges from *The Oresteia* confirms the teaching of Robert Bellah. "[T]he right always involves constraint; laws must be enforced. But we are drawn to the good by love" (Bellah, 2003, p. 47). In the closing scene of *The Eumenides*, the Athenian justice system, supported by the passionate powers of the Kindly Ones, but ruled by Apollonian logic, takes the form of a torchlight civic procession, a ritual dance which includes all citizens. In that orderly march, the rules for each citizen's civic participation are clear, but each person is motivated to contribute out of devotion to family, tribe, and polis. Law like love.

Shakespeare: *Measure for Measure*

Shakespeare's preoccupation with law is found in many of his plays, but his late dark comedy, *Measure for Measure*, casts the longest shadows over legal institutions. But despite the darkness, the play culminates in a trial which, similar to that in *The Eumenides*, enacts the union of law and love.

Using as his source the familiar folk tale of the "Unjust Judge," Shakespeare sets his scene in Renaissance Vienna, a city sunk in moral decay. Sexual license abounds: not only is prostitution rampant, but even the institution of marriage is threatened. The law prohibiting fornication has been unenforced for over 10 years. Something must be done.

As the play opens, the Duke announces the appointment of a new judge, the youthful Angelo, and an assistant magistrate, old Escalus. It seems that pressing political matters require the Duke's attention abroad. These judges will take his place and strictly enforce the law until his return. But the Duke has more in mind than using surrogates to clean up the city; he slips off to the monastery where, aided by Friar Thomas, he disguises himself as "Friar Lodowic." The Duke plans to see for himself whether young Angelo is up to the task of enforcing the law again in Vienna. In his Friar's disguise, he becomes the "Duke of dark corner."

The Duke's civics experiment doesn't take long to enact. Angelo's first case involves a violation of Vienna's moribund statute against fornication, a capital crime. The defendant, Claudio, has impregnated his betrothed, Juliet, and although they are bound by a civil contract, their nuptials are not yet solemnized in Church. Under a strict reading of the statute, Claudio is guilty. Angelo knows the law and judges accordingly:

> Angelo: See that Claudio
> Be executed by nine tomorrow morning;
> Bring him his confessor, let him be prepared;
> For that's the utmost of his pilgrimage.
> (Shakespeare, II, i, 33–36)

All is not lost. Claudio sends for his sister, Isabella, a religious Novice who is in the process of entering the Poor Clares, the strictest order of Catholic nuns. Upon learning of her brother's death sentence, she rushes from the convent to Angelo's courtroom to make an appeal. After a tumid start, she warms to the task, pressing the icy judge with a string of arguments: Condemn the sin, not the sinner. Mercy is man's greatest virtue. Many have committed this crime; none have died for it. Do not abuse your power; a proud man is dressed in a little brief authority. Ask yourself whether you might not have had the same feelings as Claudio. If so, put yourself in his shoes.

Angelo at first rejects each point, but then tells Isabella to return the next morning while he "bethinks himself." He has been moved, but not in a way Isabella intends. Angelo's icy heart has been melted and, to his own amazement, he finds himself in love with Isabella, taken over by passion. He does, indeed, find himself in Claudio's shoes.

When Isabella returns, Angelo is prepared to reverse himself—upon conditions. After Isabella fails to follow Angelo's subtle suggestion that Isabella might save her brother's life if she ". . . lay down the treasures of her body," he comes to the point:

Angelo:	Plainly conceive, I love you.
Isabella:	My brother did love Juliet,
	And you tell me that he shall die for 't
Angelo:	He shall not, Isabel, if you give me love.
	(Shakespeare, II, ix, 140–144)

Although shocked by this proposition from "the unjust judge" and confronted with a *Hobson's choice*, Isabel rejects Angelo's offer, electing to preserve her chastity even at the cost of Claudio's life. Outraged, she rushes off to the prison to tell him the sad outcome of her appeal, to ready him for death.

Coincidentally, when Isabella arrives the Duke-Friar is visiting the prisoners and overhears the anguished exchange between Isabella and Claudio. He intercepts Isabella as she is leaving the prison and, after disclosing that he heard her recount Angelo's proposition, tells her that Angelo himself, like her own brother, was betrothed. The woman in question, Mariana, was abandoned, however, because her dowry was lost at sea. Still, Angelo is legally bound to her and, therefore, if she, instead of Isabella, should sleep with Angelo, it would be no sin. The Duke-Friar tells Isabella to go back to Angelo, accept the proposition, but only on condition that the encounter be in the dark and brief. Meanwhile, the Duke-Friar will explain matters to Mariana and make the necessary arrangements for the "bed trick." Isabella accepts the holy Friar's counsel.

The switch goes as planned. The next morning, the Duke-Friar goes to the prison expecting that, as promised, Angelo will send an order to release Claudio. To his dismay, Angelo has not only reneged, he has ordered Claudio beheaded at an earlier hour, with the head to be delivered to him. The Duke-Friar again reacts to the crisis with a scheme; he convinces the Provost to stay Claudio's execution, but proceed with that of Barnardine, another condemned prisoner whose beheading is long overdue. In a hilarious twist, however, Barnardine refuses execution, claiming that he is just too hung over for such an activity. Neither the Provost, nor the Duke-Friar can talk him into it. Fortunately, it turns out that Ragozine, a notorious pirate, has conveniently died in the prison of natural causes that same night. His head is disguised to look like Claudio and sent to Angelo. The Duke-Friar's "head trick" spares Claudio.

Finally, the civics experiment is over. The Duke decides that it is time to put Angelo, and others, on trial. He sends word that he will return the next day; Angelo is to assemble the townspeople and give notice that anyone with a complaint about his judging will be heard. But Shakespeare has one more trick. In a shocking and inexplicable scene just before the Duke arrives, the Duke-Friar subjects Isabella to a cruel lie by telling her that although Angelo slept with Mariana, thinking she was Isabella, he broke his promise and executed Claudio. Her only comfort, says the Duke-Friar, is that the Duke is returning and Isabella can come forward with the truth about Angelo's double dealing. She can seek justice.

In the closing act, the Duke enters the city and takes his place on the dias between Angelo and Escalus. No sooner has he congratulated them for their good service than Isabella pushes through the crowd shouting for "justice, justice, justice, justice!" She recounts Claudio's case and Angelo's crimes: "Murderer . . . adulterous thief . . . hypocrite . . . virgin violator." But when Angelo denies the charge, the Duke turns on Isabella and, after being told about a suspicious Friar, he expresses grave doubts about her case. The Friar must be behind her outrageous claims. Noting that, after all, Angelo is renowned for his virtue, he turns the case over to Angelo to judge:

> Duke: Come, cousin Angelo
>   In this I'll be impartial; be you judge
>   Of your own cause.
>   (Shakespeare, V, i, 190–191)

As the trial continues, Mariana comes forward and testifies against Angelo. But when Angelo again denies any wrongdoing, the Duke orders that "this Friar Lodowick" be found and brought to the trial. He must have put the women up to these slanderous accusations. The

Duke then says he will leave the matter in his judges' hands and leaves. Shortly after the Duke departs, Friar Lodowick appears and faces the harsh accusations. But when Angelo orders him arrested and the Friar is roughly seized, his cowl falls back revealing the Duke. Amid the towns peoples' shocked silence, the Duke assumes the Judge's seat while Angelo drops to his knees, confessing his guilt. In response, the Duke orders Angelo to marry Mariana immediately, then return for sentencing.

The Duke proceeds to mete out justice:

> The very mercy of the law cries out
> Most audible, even from his proper tongue,
> 'An Angelo for Claudio, death for death'
> Haste still pays haste, and leisure answers leisure;
> Like doth quit like, and measure still for measure.
> (Shakespeare, V, i, 404–408)

But before Angelo is led off to execution, his new wife begs for his life. The Duke responds like Angelo in Claudio's case, telling Isabella the death sentence is "definitive." As Auden's judge would say. "The law is the law."

In this moment of crisis, Mariana desperately turns to Isabella, the other victim of Angelo's crimes:

> Mariana: Isabel,
>   Sweet Isabel, do yet but kneel by me;
>   Hold up your hands, say nothing, I'll speak all.
>   They say, best men are molded out of faults,
>   And, for the most, become much more the best
>   For being a little bad. So may my husband.
>   O Isabel, will you not lend a knee?
>   (Shakespeare, V, i, 491–497)

Now the reason for the Duke's false report of Claudio's death emerges. Isabella's commitment to Christ's core teaching is put to the ultimate test. Will she show compassion for the "unjust judge," her brother's killer? Isabella is frozen during the "greatest pause in Shakespeare." Then, finally, she drops to her knees and begs for Angelo's life. The Duke is persuaded, grants clemency and gives Mariana back her husband. And, like Angelo, he too is moved by

Isabella's beauty. He ends the trial, and the play, by offering her his hand in marriage.

In Vienna, the laws regulating sexual relations have been ineffective and renewed enforcement efforts have only created new, vexing problems. Indeed, not even the Judge can carry out the law when confronted with his own sexual passions. The answer is not chastity; the populace cannot follow Isabella into the convent. Indeed, even she discovers that her devotion to moralistic rules runs counter to the law of love. She learns to temper law with mercy, even when she has every reason to insist on strict enforcement. We assume that she will marry the Duke, rather than join the Poor Clares.

The metanarrative in *Measure for Measure* links law and love in the institution of marriage. Rather than depend upon statutes prohibiting sex under pain of death, the institution of marriage legitimizes sexual relations. The marriage contract—in the play it is described as a double contract, one private, the other communal—constitutes law supported by love. And only love is the real enforcer of marriage law. So, in the last act, marriages end Vienna's plague of sexual license and revive the city's moral life.

Thus, Shakespeare's play ends by dramatizing the analogy between law and love. Just as laws must be fairly and equally applied "measure for measure," so also must love be reciprocated between husband and wife, and within families. Just as law must be flexibly applied to produce justice, marriage obligations must be tempered by spousal forgiveness. As both Mariana and Isabella argue at the end of Angelo's trial, even judges sometimes fail to keep their promises or follow the law. But "best men are molded out of faults." Neither a marriage, nor a community, can survive without compassion. Isabella's earlier argument to Angelo links law and love:

> No ceremony that to great ones 'longs,
> Not the king's crown nor deputed sword,
> The marshal's truncheon nor the judge's robe,
> Become them with one half so good a grace
> As mercy does.
> (Shakespeare, II, ii, 78–81)

As was true in Aeschylus's Athens, when the Furies' simple rule of revenge ("an eye for an eye") was subsumed into a judicial system based on the complex interplay of law and mercy, so also in

Shakespeare's Vienna. Although "sword" and "truncheon" play a role in maintaining civic order, the life of the community depends upon the good grace of mercy. Law like love.

Conclusion

In *How to Read a Poem*, Edward Hirsch (1999) explains that a simile, in contrast to a metaphor, maintains compatibility between unlike things, but also draws attention to their differences. "There is a digressive impulse in a simile that keeps extending out to take in new things" (pp. 308-309). According to Hirsch, a simile is a form of analogical thinking; the reader participates in making meaning by establishing, in the reader's own imagination, the nature of the previously unseen analogy. The reader must evaluate the aptness of the unexpected resemblance.

Is law like love? Does that "timid similarity" open analogically outward in the contexts of *The Eumenides* and *Measure for Measure*? My experience with teaching this literature to law students, even those who are habituated to dialogical analysis, supports affirmative answers. As we explore the literary analogies, they begin to see beyond the instrumental purposes of law, to engage a larger, more complicated, vision. Indeed, our class discussions and their essays testify to the power of metanarrative. As they report on the "aptness of unexpected resemblance," on the connections between law as pronounced and law as lived, they consistently draw insight from themselves and each other. Together they find, through the literature, a greater sense of who they are and what their life in the law might be: imagining justice.

REFERENCES

Aeschylus. (1977). *The Oresteia*. In R. Fagles (Trans.). Penguin Books.

Auden, W. H. (1991). *Collected Poems*. In E. Mendelson (Ed.). Vintage International.

Bellah, R. N. (2003). "On being Catholic and American." In M.K. McCullough (Ed.), *Fire and Ice: Imagination and Intellect in the Catholic Tradition* (pp. 31–48). Scranton, PA: University of Scranton Press.

Hirsch, E. (1999). *How to Read a Poem: And Fall in Love With Poetry*. New York: Harcourt Brace & Co.

Shakespeare, W. (1994). *Measure for Measure*. In N.W. Bawcutt (Ed.). Oxford, England: Oxford University Press.

Catastrophic Grace: Flannery O'Connor and the Catholic Imagination

Sharon Locy

The short fiction of Flannery O'Connor appears frequently in anthologies used in introductory college literature courses. How these stories are taught in secular institutions would be an interesting study; their vision is peculiarly Catholic and, even in that respect, peculiar in the sense of being eccentric. It is hard to imagine how they can be read and understood without attention to O'Connor's development of them as sacramental, particularly as analogues for the sacrament of penance. Three frequently anthologized O'Connor stories that illustrate this particular sacramental vision are "A Good Man Is Hard to Find" (1953), "Everything That Rises Must Converge" (1961), and "Revelation" (1964).

While the present designation for the sacrament of penance is the sacrament of reconciliation, it must be said that such terminology is connotatively much too soft for what occurs in O'Connor's fiction. Her characters are hardly reconciled to God—or to themselves. For them the access to grace is an identity-destroying catastrophe in which their sinfulness is scoured out of them, burned away, or blown out explosively. It is an act of divine violence much more consistent with the emotional connotation of the word penance than of reconciliation. Her purged penitents unwillingly move toward their salvation with "shocked and altered faces [showing] that even their virtues were being burned away" (O'Connor, 1988, p. 654).

Lecturing at Georgetown in 1963 on "The Catholic Novelist in the Protestant South," O'Connor discussed the "misunderstanding of what the operation of grace *can* look like in fiction":

> The reader wants his grace warm and binding, not dark and disruptive. He is very busy always looking for some new Doctor Pangloss who will assure him that this is the best of all possible worlds. The word that occurs again and again in his demands of the novel is the word 'positive.' He seems to assume that what the writer writes about will follow a broad general attitude he has about the goodness of

113

creation and our redemption and resurrection in Christ.
There may be writers whose genuine vocation it is to doth-
is. But it is not a vocation that can be demanded of every
Catholic writer. These truths may serve for others simply as
a light in which evil is seen more closely. (O'Connor, 1988,
p. 862)

O'Connor adds that since ". . . [we] live now in an age which
doubts both fact and value, which is moved this way and that by
momentary convictions, and which regards religion as a purely private
matter," it is the job of the Catholic writer to counteract the "heresy"
of the feel-good "book club" mentality of those who ask the writer to
"lift up his heart" (O'Connor, 1988, pp. 862–863). The Catholic
writer, she asserts, must underscore the high cost of the "redemptive
act" for the reader whose "sense of evil is deluded or lacking altogether;" such a reader "has forgotten the *price* of restoration. He has forgotten the cost of truth, even in fiction" (O'Connor, 1988, p. 863).

O'Connor's fiction does present killers, and liars, and cheats
of every description, but the protagonists of "A Good Man Is Hard to
Find," "Everything That Rises Must Converge," and "Revelation" are
more subtly guilty. They are characters who fail to recognize their sin
as sin. They revel in self-righteousness, loving the sin that stands
between them and God. Convinced of their own virtue, they are resist-
ant to ordinary remorse and amendment. They must have their
"virtues" violently "burned away" before they can enter the kingdom
of heaven (O'Connor, 1988, p. 654). Each story presents an epiphany
in which the protagonist's sins are revealed, then violently purged,
sometimes at the very moment the soul is being blasted into eternity.

In each of these three stories the medium, or agent, or "occasion of grace" is someone who will not accept grace for him- or herself; there is a kind of violent "recoil," to use O'Connor's own word
(O'Connor, 1988, p. 1150). In the "recoil," the grace rejected by the
agent rebounds on the penitent soul, who is both saved and destroyed
by it. The most obvious example is the action of The Misfit in "A
Good Man Is Hard to Find" (1953). The Misfit, an escaped convict on
a killing spree, encounters the Bailey family, whose car has just over-
turned and landed them in a ditch. Talking frantically to save her own
life, the Grandmother tells him, "'I know you're a good man at heart.
I can just look at you and tell.' 'Nome,' he answers, 'I ain't a good
man'" (O'Connor, 1988, p. 147). He is, in fact, a man who blames

Christ for having "'thrown [sic] everything off balance'" by his incarnation and suffering (O'Connor, 1988, p. 151). In The Misfit's theology, Christ demands either complete fidelity or total rejection. He tells the frightened old woman:

> Jesus was the only One that ever raised the dead . . . and He shouldn't have done it. He thrown everything off balance. If He did what He said, then it's nothing for you to do but throw away everything and follow Him, and if He didn't, then it's nothing for you to do but enjoy the few minutes you got left the best way you can—by killing somebody or burning down his house or doing some other meanness to him. No pleasure but meanness. (O'Connor, 1988, p. 152)

Since The Misfit "wasn't there" when Jesus performed his miracles, he cannot believe in Him. "'It ain't right I wasn't there,' he says, 'because if I had of been there I would of known. . . . I would of known and I wouldn't be like I am now'" (O'Connor, 1988, p. 152). According to The Misfit, Jesus has caused him to opt for "meanness."

The Grandmother, perfectly described by one critic as "foolish, xenophobic, racially condescending, and self-righteously banal" (Orvell, 1991, p. 130), has her perceptions of the world and herself "thrown out of balance" by The Misfit. In a flash, "her head cleared for an instant," and she sees him as 'one of my babies. You're one of my own children!'" She reaches out to touch him, and "The Misfit sprang back as if a snake had bitten him and shot her three times through the chest" (O'Connor, 1988, p. 152). In the moment of her grace, The Misfit rejects the love and compassion she offers. O'Connor, writing to Andrew Lytle (4 February 1960), says: "It's the moment of grace for her anyway—a silly old woman—but it leads him to shoot her. This moment of grace excites the devil to frenzy" (O'Connor, 1988, p. 1121). In another letter (28 March 1961), to an unnamed teacher who, with his students, has grossly misread the story, O'Connor notes that "it is the fact that the old lady's gesture is the result of grace that makes it right that The Misfit shoot her. Grace is never received warmly. Always a recoil, or so I think" (O'Connor, 1988, p. 1148).

The Misfit, in spite of his rejection of the grace himself, recognizes that he has been the Grandmother's deliverer, that her death has been her salvation (Orvell, 1991, p. 174): "'She would of been a good woman . . . if it had been somebody to shoot her every minute of her life'" (O'Connor, 1988, p. 153).

O'Connor's narrative is cleverly designed to include the reader in that moment of shocking reversal. Her design is to "clobber" the reader along with the protagonist: "You can't clobber any reader while he is looking," she writes to a friend. "You divert his attention, then you clobber him, and he never knows what hit him" (Brinkmeyer, 1989, p. 178). She sets up the stories with what seem to be obvious targets of satire, to which the reader is invited to feel superior. Then, in dramatic shifts in the action and tone, she pulls the narrative rug from under the feet of the complacent, complicitious reader, effectively "clobbering" him with his own shortcomings.

In "A Good Man Is Hard to Find," for example, the story begins as a broadly comic rendition of the family car trip from hell, featuring two unpleasant and rude children, the Grandmother, her son Bailey who "didn't have a naturally sunny disposition" (O'Connor, 1988, p. 141), his wife "whose face was as broad and innocent as a cabbage" (O'Connor, 1988, p. 137), and a small baby—not to mention Pitty Sing, a cat the Grandmother has hidden in a basket because Bailey "didn't like to arrive at a motel with a cat" (O'Connor, 1988, p. 138). It is all too easy for the reader to laugh at and feel superior to these people, particularly to the Grandmother, whose consciousness is the center of the narration, making her shortcomings all too obvious. Her attachment to a past that probably never was, her pretensions to gentility and good humor (while manipulating events to get her own way), her relentless cheerfulness and instruction—all these things invite readers to think they have a handle on O'Connor's critique of the woman and her unattractive family. Even the accident, precipitated by the cat, is funny:

> "But nobody's killed," June Star said with disappointment
> as the grandmother limped out of the car, her hat still
> pinned to her head but the broken front brim standing up at
> a jaunty angle and the violet spray hanging off the side.
>   (O'Connor, 1988, p. 145)

Only with the arrival of The Misfit and his henchmen does the tone change. As, one-by-one, the family members are taken off into the woods and shot, the Grandmother argues with The Misfit for her life. In their discussion it is clear that her sense of the divine is thin and perfunctory: "'If you would pray . . . Jesus would help you,' she tells him but her own appeals to the Lord 'sounded as if she might be cursing.'" (O'Connor, 1988, pp. 150–151). The Misfit, on the other hand, has seriously examined his religious beliefs, and, warped as they are, they are neither shallow nor comforting. He is essentially correct in his understanding of Christ as having thrown the world off balance. He shatters the Grandmother's superficial beliefs, and in an instant she recognizes their essential kinship; in a gesture of love, she reaches out to him: "'Why you're one of my babies. You're one of my own children!'" (O'Connor, 1988, p. 152). Rejecting her love, The Misfit shoots her, but in doing so he seems to realize that he has not accomplished the restoration of "balance," the aim of his meanness. Earlier he has asked, "'Does it seem right to you, lady, that one is punished a heap and another ain't punished at all?'" (O'Connor, 1988, p. 151). Now, like Hamlet realizing that killing Claudius when he is praying might send him to the afterlife purged of his guilt—"'am I then revenged,/To take him in the purging of his soul,/When he is fit and seasoned for his passage?'" (pp. 84–86).—The Misfit recognizes that he has delivered the old woman to the heaven he has rejected. "'It's no real pleasure in life,' he tells one of his accomplices, not even in meanness" (O'Connor, 1988, p. 153).

In her death the Grandmother ceases to be "a silly old woman" to be laughed at; she has made her choice in what Jefferson Humphries (1983) calls "a searing intuition of the sacred" and has moved "out of the old-womanly selfishness which has defined her character throughout the story. . . . She reaches such a clarity of vision that she is able to recognize what she and The Misfit have in common, and to pity his hopelessness" (p. 118).

In letters to John Hawkes (26 December 1959 and 14 April 1960) O'Connor also considers the possibility that The Misfit himself, although he has rejected the grace offered him by the Grandmother, is "redeemable" (O'Connor, 1988, p. 1108). In the April 14, 1960, letter she writes:

> Grace, to the Catholic way of thinking, can and does use as its medium the imperfect, purely human, and even hypocritical. Cutting yourself off from Grace is a very decided matter requiring a real choice, act of will, and affecting the very ground of the soul. The Misfit is touched by the Grace that comes through the old lady when she recognizes him

as her child, as she has been touched by the Grace that comes through him in his particular suffering. His shooting her is a recoil, a horror at her humanness, but after he has done it and cleaned his glasses, the Grace has worked in him and he pronounces his judgment: she would have been a good woman if *he* had been there every moment of her life. (p. 1125)

The readers, too, must now choose. O'Connor has, in effect, put a gun to their heads, "clobbered" them. To have ". . . somebody there to shoot [you] every minute of [your] life" is a violent and graphic analogue for an awareness of one's sinfulness and the need to repent and amend one's life.

In "Everything That Rises Must Converge" (1961), the title story of O'Connor's last (and posthumous) collection (1964), the clobbering of the reader is even more ingenious. Immature readers, or those just not paying enough attention, are easily seduced into misinterpreting O'Connor's target. College students—who know intimately how embarrassing and benighted their parents can be—frequently empathize so completely with the young protagonist, Julian, that they miss O'Connor's rather obvious clues that *he* is the character who must repent his sins and throw his old life away. His mother is an easier target and so much easier to observe critically. Yet we observe her through Julian's cold and cynical eyes, with much of what she says and all of what she thinks delivered through indirect discourse, through her son's superior and loveless consciousness; it is a method of portraying her—a kind of nasty ventriloquism—that makes her appear both as bad as and worse than she really is. In characterizing his mother the way he does, Julian reveals his own dark self.

Julian's mother is, of course, worthy of criticism. She is one of a parade of O'Connor characters (almost always women) who can be described as "gracious racists." A member of a family that once was prosperous and had a plantation and slaves, she thinks the world is now a "mess," with "the bottom rail . . . on the top" (O'Connor, 1988, p. 487). The rising of the black race is not progress in her estimation, but if they must rise they should do it ". . . on their own side of the fence" (p. 488). She prides herself on her ability to "be gracious to anybody" because, she says, "I know who I am" (p. 487). Such a character in an O'Connor story is bound to get her comeuppance.

Her "lesson" begins comically when a large black woman, wearing a hat identical to hers, gets on the bus with her small son. The hideous hat—which has represented to Julian's mother her individuality, good taste, and superiority—symbolizes the "rise" of the black woman and her "convergence" with Julian's mother; as the black woman takes the seat next to Julian and her small son climbs into the seat next to Julian's mother, Julian notes with pleasure that his mother and the black woman ". . . had, in a sense, swapped sons" (O'Connor, 1988, p. 495). Julian has a momentary wave of sympathy for his mother when he thinks her illusions are about to be destroyed, but his vindictiveness overrides this positive feeling:

> She turned her eyes on him slowly. The blue in them seemed to have turned a bruised purple. For a moment he had an uncomfortable sense of her innocence, but it lasted only a second before principle rescued him. Justice entitled him to laugh. His grin hardened until it said to her as plainly as if he were saying aloud: Your punishment exactly fits your pettiness. This should teach you a permanent lesson. (O'Connor, 1988, p. 496)

However, Julian's mother seems less affected by the identical hats than the black woman is; she begins to see the obvious humor in the situation: "With a sinking heart, he saw incipient signs of recovery on her face and realized that this was going to strike her suddenly as funny and was going to be no lesson at all" (O'Connor, 1988, p. 496). The real lesson, the "permanent" one, comes as a result of Julian's mother's condescension to the woman's child; as they all leave the bus, she offers the child a penny. The child's mother ". . . explode[s] like a piece of machinery that had been given one ounce of pressure too much" (O'Connor, 1988, p. 498):

> Julian saw the black fist swing out with the red pocketbook. He shut his eyes and cringed when he heard the woman shout, "He don't take nobody's pennies!" When he opened his eyes, the woman was disappearing down the street with the little boy staring wide-eyed over her shoulder. Julian's mother was sitting on the sidewalk. (O'Connor, 1988, p. 498)

While this seems to be one of those violent purgative actions that destroys the penitent's old self and creates a new one, it might be argued that it does not exactly have that effect on Julian's mother. To be sure, she is devastated. And it becomes clear as the scene unfolds that this act of violence precipitates her death; she has suffered a stroke, and as the story ends, she is dying on the pavement. But in spite of Julian's desire to drive home the lesson he thinks his mother should learn by relentlessly haranguing her as she stumbles down the street, she dies clinging to the images of her past. "'Tell Grandpa to come get me,' she pleads; 'Tell Caroline [the black woman who was her nurse in better days] to come get me.'" It is Julian for whom the permanent lesson is prepared. The death of his mother propels Julian out of his old sinful self "into the world of guilt and sorrow" (O'Connor, 1988, p. 500).

Joyce Carol Oates (1973), in an essay on this last O'Connor collection, writes: "When the intellectual Julian suffers the real loss of his mother, the real Julian emerges; his self-pitying depression vanishes at once; the faith he had somehow lost 'in the midst of his martyrdom' is restored" (Oates, 1973, p. 49). Although Oates develops the connection between these stories and Teilhard de Chardin's concept of the spiritual evolution of man and his convergence with the divine—from which O'Connor took her title—she prefers to interpret the experiences of O'Connor's characters as psychological rather than religious, even while acknowledging that O'Connor ". . . would certainly refute me in saying this." This is logical for one who appreciates O'Connor's work but does not "share [her] specific religious beliefs" (Oates, 1973, p. 49).

However, as unfashionable as it may be to accept the author's word for what his or her intention is, O'Connor's explicit discussion of her own fiction makes it impossible to see the meaning of her work as anything but religious. She writes, in a letter to Cecil Dawkins (19 June 1957), that all of her fiction ". . . concerns specifically Christ and the Incarnation. . . . That is the fulcrum that lifts my particular stories" (O'Connor, 1988, p. 1035). Her disdain, even outrage, at the merely psychological interpretations of her work appears frequently in her correspondence. O'Connor always makes the distinction between the realistic and the spiritual, and she warns against trying to theorize philosophically about her work. "Don't mix up thought-knowledge with felt-knowledge," she writes to Dawkins on 6 September 1962 (O'Connor, 1988, p. 1174).

Julian's sin in "Everything That Rises Must Converge" is his intellectual pride and his inability to feel love and genuine empathy. He fancies himself free of his mother's racial prejudices, but he views Negroes ("the better types") not as individuals but as weapons in his desire to teach his mother a lesson; he will bring home ". . . some distinguished Negro professor or lawyer" or, better yet, ". . . a beautiful suspiciously Negroid woman" to shock ". . . the dwarf-like proportions of her moral nature." It is no wonder then that ". . . he had never been successful at making any Negro friends" (O'Connor, 1988, pp. 494-495.) He prides himself on his mental development and his ability to be emotionally detached (so he thinks) from his mother:

> In spite of going to only a third-rate college, he had, on his own initiative, come out with a first-rate education; in spite of growing up dominated by a small mind, he had ended up with a large one; in spite of all her foolish views, he was free of prejudice and unafraid to face fact. Most miraculous of all, instead of being blinded by love for her as she was for him, he had cut himself emotionally free of her and could see her with complete objectivity. He was not dominated by his mother. (O'Connor, 1988, p. 492)

He is, of course, completely dominated by his desire to punish his mother—not for any real wickedness but for the love and goodness she has extended to him and for which he feels the pressure of obligation. She has suffered for him, but he imagines himself a martyr to her needs; the first image O'Connor gives of Julian is of him ". . . waiting like Saint Sebastian for the arrows to begin piercing him" (1988, p. 485). He wants the punishment of his mother to be permanent and violent: "At that moment he could with pleasure have slapped her as he would have slapped a particularly obnoxious child in his charge" (O'Connor, 1988, p. 494). Julian's epiphany comes only at the very end of the story, when he realizes that his mother is dying. Overwhelmed by loss—and, at last, love—he calls out to her: "'Mother! . . . Darling, sweetheart . . . Mamma! Mamma!'" He is "[swept] back to her, postponing from moment to moment his entry into the world of guilt and sorrow" (O'Connor, 1988, p. 500). The last words of the story suggest that the rest of Julian's life will be a version of purgatory on earth—a life-long repentance for his sins.

This is the fate of the protagonist of "Revelation" (1964) as well—"Purrrgatory [sic]," O'Connor writes to her friend Maryat Lee (O'Connor, 1988, p. 1207). This last O'Connor story, so wonderfully crafted even as she is dying of complications from lupus, is the perfect analogue for the sacrament of penance. The protagonist, Ruby Turpin, is supremely self-satisfied, certain of her place among the saved. She sees her earthly success as proof of her election:

> "If it's one thing I am," Mrs. Turpin said with feeling, "it's grateful. When I think who all I could have been besides myself and what all I got, a little of everything, and a good disposition besides, I just feel like shouting, 'Thank you, Jesus, for making everything the way it is!' It could have been different!" For one thing, somebody else could have got Claud. At the thought of this she was flooded with gratitude and a terrible pang of joy ran through her. "Oh, thank you, Jesus, Jesus, thank you!" she cried aloud. (O'Connor, 1988, p. 644)

Mrs. Turpin sees no reason to repent, to amend her life; her life is fine, as far as she is concerned. She and her docile husband have a prosperous farm; she is blessed with "a good disposition" and sees herself as "a respectable, hard-working, church-going woman" (O'Connor, 1988, p. 648). She is also one of those "gracious racists;" she condescends to the black workers on her farm but views them as "'Idiots!': 'You could never say anything intelligent to a nigger. You could talk at them but not with them'" (O'Connor, 1988, p. 650). She would, however, prefer to be a Negro—"a neat clean respectable Negro woman, herself but black"—if, "before he made her," Jesus made her choose to be either a Negro or white trash (O'Connor, 1988, p. 636). In fact, Mrs. Turpin has considerable difficulty in figuring out exactly what Jesus means when he distributes the blessings among the classes, since it is not such a surefire way of determining who the elect really are. It is not as simple as a hierarchy based solely on race or on property:

> [The] complexity of it would begin to bear in on her, for some of the people with a lot of money were common and ought to be below she and Claud and some of the people

who had good blood had lost their money and had to rent
and then there were colored people who owned their homes
and land as well. . . . Usually by the time she had fallen
asleep all the classes of people were moiling and roiling
around in her head, and she would dream they were all
crammed together in a box car, being ridden off to be put
in a gas oven. (O'Connor, 1988, p. 636)

This last image is, of course, a chilling one and an indictment
of the horror of the Holocaust and the idea of ranking races as superi-
or or inferior. Mrs. Turpin's dream, interestingly enough, suggests
that, at least subliminally, she recognizes that creating such hierarchies
is impossible and evil. But her inklings of insecurity are not enough to
shake her out of her self-satisfaction. It takes an act of violence to
make Mrs. Turpin see herself in a different way and to prepare her for
the grace of repentance.

In "Revelation" the vehicle for Mrs. Turpin's moment of
grace is a fat, ugly, acne-scarred girl aptly named Mary Grace, who,
with her stylish mother, is among those in the doctor's waiting room.
The clientele are like Mrs. Turpin's dream of the social hierarchy that
so confounds her—Mrs. Turpin and her husband Claud; the stylish
lady and her daughter; a white-trash family consisting of a grandmother, mother and child; a "lean stringy old fellow" pretending to be
asleep (O'Connor, 1988, p. 633), and a gum-chewing young woman
Mrs. Turpin cannot "place" exactly until she enters the inner office
"on red high-heeled shoes" (O'Connor, 1988, p. 638). To make the
ensemble complete, a black delivery boy comes in at one point with
colas from the drug store for the nurses (O'Connor, 1988, p. 639).

Mary Grace, a sour college student, sits reading her textbook
entitled *Human Development* and silently scowling at the occupants of
the waiting room, Mrs. Turpin in particular. The Grandmother in "A
Good Man Is Hard to Find" senses that her deliverer, The Misfit, is
someone she knows: "His face was as familiar to her as if she had
known him all her life but she could not recall who he was"
(O'Connor, 1988, p. 146). Her moment of grace is her recognition of
him, not literally as the escaped convict but figuratively as her own
child. Conversely, in "Revelation" Mrs. Turpin has an uneasy sense
that Mary Grace knows her and has singled her out for some reason:
"[The] ugly girl's eyes were fixed on Mrs. Turpin as if she had some
very special reason for disliking her" (p. 638). As Mrs. Turpin airs her

views on blacks and white trash, her own good disposition, property, and her own blessedness, ". . . she was aware that the ugly girl's peculiar eyes were still on her" (p. 639). Mary Grace seems to see right through Ruby Turpin: "She was looking at her as if she had known and disliked her all her life—all of Mrs. Turpin's life, it seemed too, not just all the girl's life. Why, girl, I don't even know you, Mrs. Turpin said silently" (p. 640).

Mary Grace even seems to respond negatively to Mrs. Turpin's unexpressed thoughts, unnerving the complacent woman and shaking her confidence in herself: "There was no doubt in her mind that the girl did know her, knew her in some intense and personal way, beyond time and place and condition" (O'Connor, 1988, p. 646).

The moment of identity-shattering violence comes after Mrs. Turpin's thankful outburst that Jesus has made her who she is and selected her, it seems, for special blessings. Mary Grace literally "throws the book" at her, hurling the psychology text at her head and then lunging at her, sinking her fingers ". . . like clamps into the soft flesh of her neck" (p. 644). Until this moment Mrs. Turpin is not very highly evolved spiritually, in de Chardin's sense; being "clobbered" by a book on human development is a nice little joke on O'Connor's part. But it is no joke for Ruby Turpin, who must now wrestle with what this action means: "'What you got to say to me?' she asked hoarsely and held her breath, waiting, as for a revelation." Mary Grace's message is, "'Go back to hell where you came from, you old wart hog'" (p. 646).

Ruby Turpin's epiphany is not immediate, although the girl's words begin to take effect before the woman's awaited revelation. Her perception of herself and her place in the universe begins to change. As she and Claud drive home she reassesses the property that once gave her such assurance of God's favor; feeling decidedly out of favor, she wonders if that property has been taken away also:

> As their pick-up truck turned into their own dirt road and made the crest of the hill, Mrs. Turpin gripped the window ledge and looked out suspiciously. The land sloped gracefully down through a field dotted with lavender weeds and at the start of the rise their small yellow frame house, with its little flower beds spread out around it like a fancy apron, sat primly in its accustomed place between two giant hickory trees. She would not have been startled to see a burnt

wound between two blackened chimneys. (O'Connor, 1988, p. 647)

While she repeatedly rejects Mary Grace's characterization—"'I am not . . . a wart hog. From hell.'"—she gradually admits to herself that the girl's message, ". . . directed only at her, brooked no repudiation" (O'Connor, 1988, p. 647). Initially this angers her, and the second to last scene of the story pits her against God Himself. Hosing down the pigs in her sanitary pig parlor, Ruby Turpin asks the hard questions: "'How am I a hog and me both? How am I saved and from hell too?'" (p. 652). Why, she roars out to God, didn't Mary Grace's message go to someone else: "'There was plenty of trash there. It didn't have to be me'" (p. 652). In her fury she asks God, "'Who do you think you are?'" (p. 653) In a letter to Maryat Lee (15 May 1964) O'Connor admits to admiring Mrs. Turpin: "You got to be a very big woman to shout at the Lord across a pig pen" (p. 1207). It is perhaps this strength of character that gives her the courage to accept the vision she is about to be given. Joyce Carol Oates (1973) notes, "It is rare in O'Connor that an obtuse, unsympathetic character ascends to a higher level of self-awareness; indeed, she shows more courage than O'Connor's intellectual young men" (Oates, 1973, p. 51). The vision Mrs. Turpin receives does require courage to accept, because it shakes the very foundations of her self-definition. In it she sees ". . . a vast swinging bridge extending upward from the earth through a field of living fire," and on that bridge is a parade of souls "rumbling toward heaven" (O'Connor, 1988, p. 654). The procession of the saved is in reverse order of her hierarchy of the blessed:

> There were whole companies of white-trash, clean for the first time in their lives, and bands of black niggers in white robes, and battalions of freaks and lunatics shouting and clapping and leaping like frogs. And bringing up the end of the procession was a tribe of people whom she recognized at once as those who, like herself and Claud, had always had a little of everything and the God-given wit to use it right. . . . They were marching behind the others with great dignity, accountable as they had always been for good order and common sense and respectable behavior. . . . Yet she could see by their shocked and altered faces that even their virtues were being burned away. (O'Connor, 1988, p. 654)

Like the respectable people in her vision, Mrs. Turpin realizes that her so-called virtues are of no account; they are "burned away" (O'Connor, 1988, p. 654).

Of the protagonists in these three stories, Ruby Turpin has been shown making the most conscious examination of her conscience, and her penance is the most clearly suggested at the end of the narrative. The Grandmother in "A Good Man Is Hard to Find" receives her absolution immediately—and definitively—in her death; Julian, in "Everything That Rises Must Converge," is only on the brink of his, ". . . postponing from moment to moment his entry into the world of guilt and sorrow" (O'Connor, 1988, p. 500). Ruby Turpin, at the end of "Revelation," seems to realize that her experience commits her to a lifelong repentance. She has her eyes ". . . fixed unblinking on what lay ahead" (p. 654). We are to understand that this is not merely a momentary revelation. Writing to Maryat Lee (15 May 1964) a few months before her death, O'Connor comments on Mrs. Turpin's understanding of her vision: "She gets the vision. Wouldn't have been any point in that story if she hadn't. . . . And that vision is purgatorial. Purrrgatory [sic]—" (p. 1207).

While these three stories appear frequently in college fiction anthologies, they are very difficult for college students to understand, even in the Catholic university, where students might be expected to read them as expressions of a thoroughly religious imagination. In a lecture given in 1963, O'Connor expressed the feeling that the ". . . sense of evil [was] deluded or lacking altogether" in her own day (O'Connor, 1988, p. 863). This is probably even more true today, when children being instructed to make their first confessions are taught about "wrong choices" rather than "sin." O'Connor resists such a softening of the idea of evil. Her vision is not a comfortable one, and her view of the vocation of the Catholic writer is unsparing. In her lecture on the Catholic novelist in the south (1963) she emphasizes the need for the Christian storyteller to persist in pointing out ". . . the price of restoration . . . the cost of truth, even in fiction" (O'Connor, 1988, p. 863).

REFERENCES

Asals, F. (1982). "The double." In H. Harold Bloom (Ed.), *Flannery O'Connor* (1986, pp. 93–109). New York: Chelsea House.

Brinkmeyer, R. H., Jr. (1989). *The Art and Vision of Flannery O'Connor.* Baton Rouge, LA: Louisiana State University Press.

Friedman, M. J., & Lawson, L. A. (1977). *The Added Dimension: The Art and Mind of Flannery O'Connor.* New York, NY: Fordham University Press.

Humphries, J. (1983). "Proust, Flannery O'Connor and the aesthetics of violence." In H. Bloom (Ed.) *Flannery O'Connor* (1986, pp. 111–124). New York, NY: Chelsea House.

Oates, J. C. (1973). "The visionary art of Flannery O'Connor." In H. Bloom (Ed.), *Flannery O'Connor* (1986, pp. 43–53). New York, NY: Chelsea House.

O'Connor, F. (1988). *O'Connor Collected Works* (1st ed.). New York: Library of America.

Orvell, M. (1991). *Flannery O'Connor: An Introduction.* Jackson, MS: University Press of Mississippi.

The Flesh of Adam: Women, Bodies and the Sacramental Imagination

Marie Anne Mayeski

"When all things were in quiet silence, and night was in the midst of her course, your almighty Word, O Lord, leapt down from heaven from your royal throne" (Wisdom 18:14–15, *Revised English Bible*). Thus has the Catholic Church, for many centuries, sung its faith in the Incarnation during the Christmas season. What a leap, indeed, from timelessness into time, from fullness of might into fragile infancy, from pure spirit into weak and corruptible flesh. To encounter the mystery also requires a leap—of faith, of intellect, and of imagination. For Incarnation is the ultimate paradox; faith in the Word of God Incarnate affirms not only that the divine spirit is effective in human history, but that it is embodied in human flesh, which, with its weakness and constraints, is the diametrical opposite of God. One can dwell in the realm of this paradox only through an act of faith, in which intellect ignites the imagination in a flash of intuitive fire. Intellect, indeed, could reason to the necessity for such a leap; St. Anselm of Canterbury did so with clarity in the 11th century. But only imagination—a sacramental imagination—can hold together that which all logic must forever see as opposed, the spirit and the flesh.

The author of the fourth Gospel is a witness that the paradox of embodied spirit was problematic from the earliest days. Concerned that gnostic Christians have already begun to erode the salvific value of Christ's humanity, he affirms unequivocally in the Prologue that "the Word became flesh" (John 1:14), using the Greek word "sarx" to emphasize the meaty reality of Christ's flesh. In his first epistle, he repeats his emphasis: ". . . we have seen it with our own eyes, we looked upon it, and felt it with our own hands" (1John 1:1). The increasing influence of neo-platonic dualism upon Christian theology only exacerbated early gnostic tendencies to denigrate the human body; it is a scholarly commonplace that women often felt the greatest weight of this increasing negativity about the spiritual worth of human flesh. It is also generally assumed that the Middle Ages were increasingly dualistic in outlook, and thus committed to a spiritualized concept of the afterlife. Earthly realities were held completely in contempt.

Such a generalization does not, I believe, survive a close reading of individual texts. There are a great variety of points of view in medieval texts, especially in those that pre-date scholasticism. Some of the most interesting and positive theological reflections on the sacredness of the human body I have found are in the texts of early medieval women. For Dhuoda of Septimania (fl. 840), an aristocratic woman of the late Carolingian period, the biological and social reality of genealogy becomes the source of her understanding of the importance of the body. For Julian of Norwich (fl. 1340), it is the soteriological implications of the doctrine of creation. But both women arrive at a realistic appreciation of the human body as that reality, treasured by Christ, through which human solidarity is created and human selfishness redeemed. Each has exercised an active "sacramental imagination" upon the realities of her own life. For Dhuoda, it was motherhood and, her maternal obligations to form the consciences of her sons, that evoked her reflections. For Julian, her work as a spiritual director seems to have moved her to a renewed understanding of the doctrine of creation. Though separated by some 500 years, both came to use the phrase "the flesh of Adam" as a focal point for their reflections. The "flesh of Adam" connotes all that was most problematic about humanity. Flesh signifies the antithesis of spirit and, by extension, of all that is divine and eternal. It calls up images of death, corruption and pain. Adam, though he is indeed the father of all the living, was, in fact, the instrument of death and damnation. A typical motif of medieval iconography shows a gaping and skeletal Adam under the earth; from the seed in the shriveled apple in his mouth grows the cruciform tree on which Christ is hung. Yet in the sacramental imaginations of Dhuoda and Julian come a reinterpretation of "the flesh of Adam" to denote the salvific possibilities of biological maternity, the Christian importance of human solidarity, and the human body as an instrument of grace. In short, for both of these women, all human embodiment is a sacred reality.

For Dhuoda of Septimania, the related concepts of genealogy, ancestry, and inheritance were preeminently important as both theological categories and the practical framework of her world. This mother of two sons wrote a book for their formation, entitled the *Liber*

Manualis; in it, she explores the ramifications of genealogy for her sons' practical actions and for their spiritual development. Dhuoda is concerned, first of all, with the biological and material realities of genealogy and inheritance. In the Carolingian world, one's ancestors were the source of status, territory, and temporal vocation. She bids William, her older son, pray for his father's relatives for they ". . . handed down their goods to him in legitimate inheritance" (Dhuoda, 1991, p. 87). She appends to her work a full list of those relations and notes that those who have inherited the passing wealth of this world owe continual prayer for the salvation of the dead who have bequeathed it. Knowing full well that worldly power inevitably involves conflict over wealth and status, Dhuoda offers her son a moral program by which he is to negotiate the conflicting loyalties he owes to family and to his feudal lord. The Carolingian world was rife with civil and familial conflicts; Dhuoda offers her own moral understanding of how feudal and family obligations may best be honored if William fully understands his primary obligations to God (Mayeski, 1995).

Biological ancestry also forms the basis on which Dhuoda assumes the role of religious teacher in William's life; she claims the privilege of being William's mother in the faith because she is also his mother in the flesh. While this may seem obvious to us, she acknowledges, in the Prologue to the *Liber*, that her attempt to teach religious doctrine to William requires justification. The Church's ban on women as religious teachers was still in force (though it acquired cracks during the Carolingian period) and Dhuoda's husband had taken her two sons away from her shortly before she began writing (presumably to insure their safety during the civil war). Since they are bereft of her physical presence, she believes she is justified in writing her teaching for them, as unconventional as that strategy was in her world. She proffers her doctrinal teaching as first diffidently (Prologue), then with more confidence as she comes to understand that a mother's knowledge of her sons' dispositions can give her words great power (Dhuoda, 1991, I,7, p. 13). Finally she generalizes her personal situation and cites other precedents and other possibilities for extending the maternal into a formal teaching role (Dhuoda, 1991, VII, 3, 1991, p. 80). She comes to see the maternal vocation—a biological one, of course—as the basis for authority in religious teaching.

Dhuoda also sees genealogy as a biblical category. Taking her cue from the concept "salvation history" and from a typological interpretation of the Jewish Scriptures, Dhuoda sees the great figures of Israelite history, especially royal and aristocratic persons, as William's ancestors in the faith. From Abraham and Isaac, David and Solomon, from Daniel counseling Baltassar and Achior advising Holofernes, William has inherited both a religious faith and a pattern of political behavior. As he must pay homage to his biological ancestors with both prayers and moral behavior, so must he honor his biblical ancestors by enacting the justice of God and by imitating their political prudence. Her use of genealogical categories here seems something less than biological but more than purely spiritual.

All this is briefly described to demonstrate that, for Dhuoda, genealogy, ancestry, and inheritance are important categories under which she discusses some of her most urgent theological material. Note, too, that her understanding of these things obviates to some degree the dualism of body and spirit, nature and grace. In fact, biological descent involves spiritual consequences and obligations; grace is transmitted equally through natural and supernatural ancestors; the social roles, which are conferred by blood and sexual union, confer religious and ecclesial obligations as well as political ones. It is not surprising, therefore, that the universal descent of humankind from "the flesh of Adam" should be a subject out of which Dhuoda draws several conclusions, both practical and theological, that are pertinent to the question of embodiment.

The context of the passage in which Dhuoda most fully develops these conclusions is important. It comes at the end of Book 4, in the course of which she has explained the application of the Beatitudes and the Gifts of the Holy Spirit to the secular and spiritual responsibilities of her son's life (Mayeski, 1995). In Chapter 9, Dhuoda entreats William to "help the poor as you are able" and in developing this idea she writes:

> It is fitting that he who accepts at no cost another's goods should offer his own for free to the extent that he can. Therefore I direct you to minister with food and drink to the needy and with clothing to the naked. May each man [sic] give away with a smile what he knows is his. It is written, "Deal thy bread to the hungry, and bring the needy

and the harbourless into thy house: when thou shalt see one naked, cover him, and despise not thy own flesh."

Here, the word "flesh" signifies the state of brotherhood in which all of us take our origin, as the first-made man himself said of her who was like him and joined to him, "This is now bone of my bones, flesh of my flesh." For "flesh," *caro*, takes its name from "to fall," *cadere*, in the sense and to the degree that the poor man as well as the rich may fall and rise again, but all are returned to dust in the end. Hence it is just that those who acquire great things through their merits should offer material sustenance and aid to such lesser persons of whom they are aware. In fraternal compassion—for those who thirst, hunger and are naked, to orphans and pilgrims, strangers and widows, and to little children and all the needy and oppressed—help them kindly, taking pity upon them whenever you see them. For if you do so, "then shall thy light break forth as the morning," and brightness shine upon your steps everywhere. Mercy and peace will never desert you, and everywhere, through all time, truth and justice shall go before thy face. (Dhuoda, 1991, IV, 9, pp. 62–63)

The opening sentence of this passage connects what Dhuoda is about to say to her general concern for the implications of ancestry. The burden of generosity falls most appropriately upon the one "who accepts at no cost another's goods," that is, upon someone who has inherited both wealth and status from others, the ancestors who have gone before and provided for their descendants through their work and their resolution of conflicts. William has not personally acquired his own wealth; having received it as a gift of his biological ancestors, he is obligated to share it generously. She quotes Isaiah 58 in support of her convictions about generous giving. Since the citation includes the word "flesh," ('caro' in the Vulgate), Dhuoda then explains how this word shapes a Christian's attitude to others, especially in the distribution of wealth.

"Flesh" refers, first of all, to the "state of brotherhood" which is a consequence of our common origin in Adam. It is the flesh of Adam, his body, that is the common physical patrimony of all humankind, and this shared bodiliness is, for Dhuoda, the basis of social responsibilities that extend to the entire human race. She cites Genesis

2:23, "you are bone of my bones, flesh of my flesh," a text used consistently to explain the God-given purpose of marriage, thus underlining that it is through sexual union sanctified in marriage that the common patrimony of the body is transmitted. In giving one of her many erroneous etymologies, she does link "flesh" to its frailty ("for 'flesh' *caro* takes its name from 'to fall,' *cadere*"), but for her the frailty of human embodiment has little or nothing to do with any religious contempt for the body. She does acknowledge the inevitability of death as a sign of the body's relative insignificance, but its frailty is also and especially related to the ordinary social rhythms of human affairs. In the temporal order, men and women sometimes rise in social importance and in riches and then they lose both again, often through no personal fault or even political failure. It was a lesson that Dhuoda saw being played out all around her throughout her life; she refers elsewhere to the way in which that cyclic wheel of fortune had affected the fate of her own family.

And so, she puts these two truths together. On the one hand, human embodiment means that all people are biologically related to one another, all are family, since all come from one set of parents through the long history of human sexual union. On the other hand, the frailty of human flesh is revealed in the inexorable rhythms of social influence; all human beings are vulnerable to the effects of changing political forces and systems, which allot great riches to some and allow many others to suffer penury. From the conjunction of these truths comes William's particular moral obligations. Having inherited the means to right the balance, not because of his own goodness but through the fortunes of blood and political inheritance, William is obligated "in fraternal compassion" to share his wealth with others, "those who thirst, hunger and are naked, to orphans and pilgrims, strangers and widows, and to little children and all the needy and oppressed" (Dhuoda, 1991, IV,9, p. 62-3). Dhuoda gives very specific content to her general moral principle; by listing the many categories of those who have a claim on William's riches, she echoes not only the Beatitudes but also the social facts of the Carolingian world. That she includes "strangers" in the list further emphasizes that William's moral responsibilities, which flow from his connection to his ancestor Adam, can admit no social or political limits.

By understanding "embodiment" under the category of ancestry and inheritance, Dhuoda has, above all, given bodiliness its full

social significance. Inheritance is a completely biological and physical reality, accomplished through sexual union and manifested
through shared physicality as well as through family connections,
money and power. But it is also the means through which we inherit
spiritual, and religious blessings, and obligations. Descendents of the
biblical people of faith, we inherit from them the conditions of the
possibility of our own faith, as well as the moral and religious insights
by which we are expected to live. Universally the descendents of
Adam, we inherit a global family with its full range of social weaknesses and a religious responsibility that is coextensive with the
human race.

When we turn to the text of Julian of Norwich, we move five
centuries ahead and to world that is significantly different, both socially and theologically. Yet she too uses the notion of "the flesh of Adam"
to explore some of the ramifications of embodiment. Julian attends
much more in her text to the human body in all its complexity than did
Dhuoda. This is, undoubtedly, a matter of the times in which she lived;
no one in 14th century England could have remained unaware of the
body's potential for pain and degradation, surrounded as they were by
the ravages of the Black Death, continual warfare, hunger, and great
poverty. It was also a time in which much of the Church's pastoral
activity was greatly influenced by the philosophical dualism that had
been inherent in Christian teaching from the beginning. Certain
aspects of Julian's life also gave her a perspective on the human body
that was at odds with the common teaching. First of all, she received
her revelations, the series of visions and insights about which she
writes, as a bodily experience; she is therefore predisposed to understand that the body can be a powerful instrument of grace. Secondly,
she was an anchorite, and in her quasi-solitary existence she had to
learn a balanced way of caring for her body as well as disciplining it;
otherwise her vocation would have been impossible to maintain over
a long period of time. Aelred of Rievaulx, for instance, in his 12th century *Rule for a Recluse*, has a great deal to say about the essential
moderation in physical austerities, which the life of a recluse requires.
Thirdly, we have external evidence that Julian functioned as a spiritual director for the 20 or so years that passed between the visions and
her definitive interpretation written down in the *Longer Version*. The
impact of her pastoral experience is evident on every page of her text
and issues about the meaning of the body, its potential for good and

ill, were important to her pastoral clients. (Margery Kempe was one of these clients and her body issues are almost legendary). For all of these reasons, Julian addresses the notion of embodiment with more conscious attention than did Dhuoda, and with greater positive sympathy than did most of her contemporaries.

A short quotation from Julian's text can illustrate both the realism and the positive appreciation with which she views human embodiment. It occurs in the sixth chapter of the *Longer Version* and reads as follows:

> A [human being] walks upright, and the food in his body is shut in as if in a well-made purse. When the time of his necessity comes, the purse is opened and then shut again, in most seemly fashion. And it is God who does this, as it is shown when he says that he comes down to us in our humblest needs. For he does not despise what he has made, nor does he disdain to serve us in the simplest natural functions of our body. . . . (Julian, 1978, p. 186)

Here Julian is referring to bowel elimination and, for her, this simple but important bodily function is, first of all, marvelously efficient. She notes how the muscular processes allow for both upright walking and bowel control, so that human behavior can be "seemly." She attributes this efficiency and respect for human dignity to God who "serves" humankind in the "simplest natural functions of our body." For Julian, God is first and foremost our Creator; indeed, her entire soteriology is refracted through the doctrine of creation. The created world, therefore, is both God's gift and the revelation of God's essential character. Her reflection on this everyday experience of her own body allows her to understand God's wisdom as an artisan of the human body and God's loving condescension toward human beings. God preserves human dignity and control even while God provides for the nourishment and the comfort of every human person.

Julian seems to realize that others in her world do not share her sensitivity to the meaning of the human body. In the last chapters of the *Longer Version* (chiefly in Chapters 53, just after the parable of the Lord and the Servant, through 63) she attempts a somewhat more systematic presentation of her anthropology. Throughout the *Showings*, she has used the language of "body" and "soul" in a conventional way. But beginning in Chapter 55, Julian begins to reflect on this language, speaking explicitly against a dualistic interpretation of it. Thus she says: "And all the gifts which God can give to the creature he has given to his Son Jesus for us, which gifts he, dwelling in us, has enclosed in him until the time that we are fully grown, our soul together with our body and our body together with our soul. Let either of them take help from the other, until we have grown to full stature as creative nature brings about; and then in the foundation of creative nature with the operation of mercy, the Holy Spirit by graces breathes into us gifts leading to endless life" (Julian, 1978, p. 287). Note here a simple attempt to describe the absolute unity of body and soul and their mutual interdependence. Note, too, that the "full stature" to which we are called to grow (the language and meaning are Pauline) is founded on "creative nature" and brought to perfection by "the operation of mercy" and the work of the Holy Spirit.

In these same chapters she also has recourse to the language of "substance" and "sensuality" in order to describe the complex reality of the human person. This theme in Julian deserves a much fuller treatment than I can give here. Suffice it to say that for Julian, "substance" and "sensuality" are, to some degree, parallel to the words "soul" and "body," they are not just fancy substitutions for the more common language. She affirms that both substance and sensuality inextricably constitute one reality, the human person.

> God is closer to us than our own soul, for he is the foundation on which our soul stands, and he is the means which keeps the substance and the sensuality together, so that they will never separate. For our soul sits in God in true rest, and our soul stands in God in sure strength and our soul is naturally rooted in God in endless love. And therefore if we want to have knowledge of our soul and communion and discourse with it, we must seek it in our Lord God in whom it is enclosed. And of this enclosing I . . . understood [that] . . . as regards our substance, it can rightly be called our soul, and as regards our sensuality, it can rightly be called our soul, and that is by the union which it has in God. (Julian, 1978, pp. 288-289)

She struggles to explain the unity of person here, designated by the word "soul." She also wants to emphasize how we are inseparable from God by nature since in God we sit, stand, are rooted and by whom we are enclosed (again, a kind of paraphrase of Paul). God is also the means, or medium, which completely unites that which we experience as two aspects of our own nature. Throughout this portion of the text, she emphasizes how, in our substance, we are in God from the beginning, and in our sensuality, we are one with Christ from the moment of his incarnation onward. Though her use of these two words in some sense mirrors the old, conventional dualism of body and soul, Julian tries carefully to affirm the complete unity of the human person; more importantly, she works to express her fundamental conviction that the human person in all its physicality is the object of God's redeeming love.

At heart, Julian's *Showings* are concerned with soteriology and the fullest expression of her soteriology is to be found in the parable of the Lord and the Servant in Chapter 51 of the *Longer Version*. There is no hint of this material in the *Shorter* and earlier version, evidence that it took her almost 20 years to come to her soteriological synthesis. In what she calls a parable (but is really an allegory), she first describes the physical vision she had of the Lord sitting on the ground and the single servant who stood before him. Between the two, there are visible bonds of affection, and in the vision the Lord sends the servant off to do a task. The servant runs to do the Lord's bidding with more eagerness than prudence and falls into a ditch. It is a simple narrative vision, but after 20 years of meditation upon it, Julian arrives at a multilayered interpretation of it that she proceeds to open out before her readers. On one level, the servant is Adam and the narrative is the story of the original fall from intimacy with God. In this meaning, Julian is most concerned with understanding how sin affects the relationship between God and Adam and is amazed that, in the vision, God does not blame Adam nor love him the less because of his sin. Equally amazing to her is that, in the vision she is given, Adam's fall is not a consequence of arrogance or willful rejection of God but of an eager, if imprudent, love. "Not only does the servant go, but he dashes off and runs at great speed, loving to do his lord's will" (Julian, 1978, p. 267). For Julian, as for Dhuoda, Adam is every man; through his flesh, Adam is the ancestor of all and so all his progeny share his situation with God. "I understood that the servant who stood before him was shown for Adam, that is to say, one man was shown at that time and his fall, so as to make it understood how God regards all [people] and their falling" (Julian, 1978, p. 270).

But if the flesh of Adam is the link between the first human being and all others, it is especially the link between Adam and Christ (yet another Pauline theme). "When Adam fell, God's Son fell; because of the true union which was made in heaven, God's Son could not be separated from Adam, for by Adam I understand all [hu]mankind" (Julian, 1978, p. 274). Julian draws out the parallels. Adam fell into a ditch which symbolizes " . . . this wretched world." Christ fell ". . . into the valley of the womb of the maiden who was the fairest daughter of Adam." Christ and Adam are one in their humanity and they are one in their earthly destiny. Adam is to be a gardener, one who digs in the earth doing ". . . the greatest labor and the hardest work there is." Christ, too, is sent to find the treasure hidden in the field which is humanity, for "human nature . . . is mixed with earth" (Julian, 1978, p. 272-275). Julian notes with amazement that the great Lord lacks something; it is this treasure of humanity saved by Christ, found in the earth and only on earth. Julian wonders why, in her vision, the Lord, great and omnipotent as he is, continues to sit upon the ground after his servant leaves, why he has only one servant and why, though all creation is his, he has no food set before him. As she weaves back and forth through the various levels of her interpretation, she begins to see that the Lord sits upon the ground because it is only when humanity is saved that creation itself, the Lord's primary work, will be complete. She notes, toward the end of the chapter, that after Christ's saving work is finished, both Father and Son "sit" triumphantly in heaven where the Holy Spirit is the love between them. The Lord has only one servant, because all humanity is one: "For in all this our good Lord showed his own Son and Adam as only one man. The strength and the goodness that we have are from Jesus Christ, the weakness and the blindness that we have are from Adam, which two were shown in the servant" (Julian, 1978, p. 275).

The food for which the Lord waits is the food brought forth from the earth and prepared by the servant, Adam-Christ. In the meaning of the food, Julian's imagination brings together the many layers of meaning she has been weaving throughout. The food is, at one and the same time, Christ's own body, His body given as food in the Eucharist, the human persons (whose nature is of the earth) and the fruits of all the work done by the sons and daughters of Adam throughout time.

It is clear that in this lengthy and richly textured interpretation of her vision of the Lord and the servant, Julian of Norwich has developed a soteriology that is both thoroughly traditional and founded on the importance of embodiment. As for Dhuoda so for Julian, the human body is that irreplaceable reality that establishes the identity between Adam, Christ and all of humanity. For Dhuoda, this becomes the basis of a moral vision; for Julian, the implications are primarily soteriological and she sees embodiment as the condition for the possibility of salvation. We are in no doubt, as we read her text, of the physical reality with which she understands embodiment; the body is no abstract symbol but the source of blood and sweat and excrement, of pain as well as of refreshment. But the same body, in which we inherit the sin of Adam and all its attendant ills, makes us one with Christ who redeems that sin, indeed all sin. In Julian's understanding of Christian revelation, then, embodiment is both the primary and fundamental gift of God and the medium through which all other divine gifts and graces are received.

The discovery of these texts has been important both for me and for my students. We live in a world that swings drunkenly between exploitation and repression in its understanding of human embodiment, with Catholic Christianity perceived to be firmly on the side of repression. Julian and Dhuoda point to an alternative way of understanding the body's full symbolic significance, a way consistent with the enduring Catholic tradition of the sacramental imagination. These texts—and others like them—may not, in themselves, change the Catholic theological world. But in the curriculum of a Catholic university they can serve to enliven a sacramental imagination and hold the Christian paradox at the center of our attention.

REFERENCES

Aelred of Rievaulx. (1971). "A rule of life for a recluse." In M. P. Macpherson (Trans.), *Treatises and the Pastoral Prayer.* Spencer, MA: Cistercian Publications.

Dhuoda of Septimania. (1975). *Liber Manualis* (P. Riche, Ed.). Paris: Editions du Cerf.

Dhuoda. (1991). *Handbook for William: A Carolingian Woman's Counsel for Her Son* (C. Neel, Trans.). Lincoln: University of Nebraska Press.

Dhuoda. (1998). *Handbook for Her Warrior Son* (M. Thiebaux, Trans.). Cambridge: Cambridge University Press.

Julian of Norwich. (1978). *Showings* (E. Colledge & J. Walsh, Trans.). New York: Dover.

Mayeski, M. A. (1995). *Dhuoda: Ninth Century Mother and Theologian.* Scranton, PA: University of Scranton Press.

Neel, C. (1991). *Handbook for William: A Carolingian Woman's Counsel for Her Son.* Lincoln, Nebraska: University of Nebraska Press.

Believing Is Seeing: *Field of Dreams* as Liturgy?

Howard Lavick

The purpose of the Loyola Marymount University President's Institute was to examine the Catholic character of the University through the lens of imagination and intellect in the Catholic tradition. I have chosen to explore this theme by using the language of film to suggest a parallel between how faith communities and the media strive to reach their audiences.

In his essay: "Liturgy as Metaphor," Mark Searle describes how religious influence is distinguished by our ability to perceive and understand. Searle, a liturgical scholar, explains that metaphor requires not only imagination, but also demands us to engage ourselves in the wonder and mystery of human existence. This, he concludes, is essential for the understanding of liturgy.

Both imagination and intellect–and, in a certain sense, belief and nonbelief—are crucial to the communication of ideas. Three phrases in particular are essential to communicating through film, television and radio: persistence of vision, believing is seeing, and suspension of disbelief. Each term can be scientifically defined, but on another level each requires a belief or faith in the unexplainable to be achieved. Each needs, in effect, both intellect and imagination.

Persistence of Vision

> [The liturgy] is neither instant gratification nor emotional catharsis. Instead the awareness of God-in-Christ which it holds out, and the encounter with him that it promises, come slowly to those who persevere and who give their eyes time to adjust to the light. (Searle, 1991, p. 116)

Persistence of vision occurs when the human eye absorbs an image of light or dark as it is transmitted through the optic nerve to the brain. This image is retained on the surface of the retina for a moment after the eye has absorbed the initial light. Were it not for this optical side-effect, the illusion of the moving image (film or video) would not be possible.

Professor Richard Blake, S.J., in his opening chapter from *Afterimage: The Indelible Catholic Imagination of Six American Filmmakers*, describes this idea of the afterimage as ". . . the image that remains or returns after the external stimulus has been withdrawn" (Blake, 2000, p. 1). For example, when a person looks at a bright object, such as a sunlit window or a flash bulb, and then closes his/her eyes, an afterimage can actually be seen for a moment after the flash has occurred. In other words, this ghost image is held on the surface of the retina momentarily before fading away. It is precisely because of this phenomenon that the perception of motion occurs during the watching of a film or video. Blake, a film critic, also uses afterimage as a unifying concept for his writing about movies and religion.

When a motion picture is projected, it is not actually showing movement. Instead, sequences of 24 individual pictures are projected each second, producing a series of still images that start-and-stop 24 times per second. Technically, what occurs is that as a reel of film moves through the projector, each frame of film is moved into the aperture where the bulb projects the image through the lens and onto the screen. Then the aperture closes and the film is advanced one frame so that the next still image can be moved into place. The aperture opens again and the next image is projected onto the screen, and so on, 24 times each second.

It is while the aperture is closed and the next frame of the picture is moved into position that persistence of vision comes into play. In fact, while the aperture is closed the screen is actually blank. However, due to persistence of vision, the eye does not see the dark screen, but instead sees the (after)image from the preceding frame. Then, when the next frame appears on the screen, the mind blends the two into a continuous series of images, thereby creating the illusion of movement. Without this effect, the individual drawings of Mickey Mouse, or the graceful dancing of Astaire and Rogers, or the breathtaking imagery of Akira Kurasawa would not come to life. On the other hand, next time you pay $8.50 for a bad movie, remember that during the two hours you were in the theater, you were paying to watch a blank screen half of the time.

Persistence of vision can mean much more than its technical description. It is through the imagination that images are given meaning, and when these images are powerful and convey religious or spiritual meanings, their message can be both dynamic and profound.

> The connection between religion and imagination, which influenced perception and behavior, is a fascinating area of inquiry . . . . Understanding the ways religion influences the imagination may help at long last to help people of conflicting faiths and those who claim no faith at all, to appreciate their differences. (Blake, 2000, p. 7)

If the eye is window to the soul, if the eye is the lens through which the meaning of ideas or beliefs is projected onto the human soul, then as purveyors of ideas, the church and media must play an increasingly important role in mankind's understanding of the world around us.

Believing is Seeing

> Metaphor demands the involvement of those who use it. The most powerful metaphors in human language are those which touch on areas of experience which clearly engage our own mystery, opening up for us the wonder and ambiguity of human existence . . . . The metaphor thus does two things: it offers insight and it lends a vocabulary in which to play out the insight. (Searle, 1991, p. 106)

Believing is seeing is a wonderful turn of phrase which best describes the influence that radio once held over people, especially before the advent of television. What is it that makes radio possible? Is it circuitry, electricity and satellites that make broadcasting a radio signal possible? Technically and intellectually yes, but it is the imagination that makes the message meaningful.

Family gatherings around the radio were a shared, communal experience consisting of individual memories. Radio listeners, captivated by the music of Glenn Miller's orchestra, could imagine the beautiful young couples dancing across the polished ballroom floor and be swept away from their own world into a more glamorous one. Tales of the *Lone Ranger* or Orson Welles's Mercury Theater broadcast of *War of the Worlds* would come alive in the mind's eye. As Americans listened to the uplifting messages broadcast by Franklin D. Roosevelt to a war-weary nation, they could imagine the President sitting resolutely at his desk and feel comforted. People were touched somehow, on a level beyond intellect. Believing was seeing.

President Roosevelt's goal was to inspire his audience to come together as a national family for the sake of the world community. In much the same way, the Church, or the Catholic university, also seeks to inspire its audience members with a core of shared beliefs that will bring them together to serve the greater good.

> The Catholic Church contributes most significantly to the life of a university by giving the university a goal beyond itself, a context for all it does . . . it enables people to live more deeply and to dream large, to develop their talents and deploy them at the world's service. This mission corresponds to a hope that many people, Catholic or not, have for their lives, the hope that we can help at least a few people to grow and be more fully themselves. A Catholic university always sees itself in light of this larger vision. (Lawton, 2003, p. 91–92)

Suspension of Disbelief

> Metaphor, in the first place, calls for a certain amount of trusting imagination, the willing suspension of disbelief . . . .We have to enter into the metaphor with a certain measure of sympathetic expectation and to linger with it until it yields up its secret. (Searle, 1991, p. 114)

In the movie *Forrest Gump*, does Tom Hanks actually shake hands with President Lyndon B. Johnson? Does Kevin Costner really conjure up long-dead baseball players for his Iowa farm in *Field of Dreams*? Of course not. Nevertheless, if we are to accept that a futuristic *Star Wars* could exist ". . . a long time ago in a galaxy far, far away," then we not only have to believe it, but in the parlance of movies, we have to suspend our disbelief.

Belief, or faith, can be construed in intellectual terms as the acceptance of that for which there is no tangible (or scientific) proof. In the world of movies, however, with increasingly sophisticated computer-enhanced special effects, who is to say what is real and what is not? What is truth and what is not? What is to be believed and what is not?

In *Field of Dreams*, some characters in the movie are able to see the resurrected baseball players, while others do not. Some of the characters come to believe in the myth, the possibility, and the dream.

They have the faith to believe in it, while others do not. Interestingly, movie audiences were divided on the credibility of this film. Some people scoffed at its Hallmark card sentimentality, while others were moved to tears at the end when the character played by Kevin Costner was reunited with his father, who had died before they could share their love. In an ironic sense, those people in the audience who ridiculed the believability of the film's premise, were unable to see the baseball players. They refused to suspend their disbelief in order to believe in the magic of the story.

Is this really so different from the connection between religious belief and imagination? We allow our imaginations to overrule our intellect, at least for a while, as we sit in the magical darkness of a movie theater. Do we not let our faith take hold while we sit in the darkened majesty of a cathedral? Our willingness to have faith in the liturgy of the Church, for example, requires not only belief, but also, at times, a willingness to suspend the disbelief of the intellect. Do miracles really occur? Was Jesus resurrected? Is there life after death? Did God speak to Moses? Does the Shroud of Turin carry the image of Jesus? Or, for that matter, is the reflection observed in the window of a car dealership in Los Angeles really the image of the Virgin Mother? Who is to say? Who is to deny?

At the dawn of this new millennium, information technologies present both opportunities and challenges. Stories, once shared around a campfire or from a pulpit, are now communicated around the world via an electronic campfire known as the Internet. Information is shared instantly and globally, but information in itself is not necessarily knowledge. And knowledge does not necessarily mean understanding.

The difference between looking and seeing, between hearing and listening, or between knowledge and understanding is the chasm between intellect and imagination. Without believing, there is no seeing. Without faith, there is no insight. Without understanding, there is no communication. And if the message is not seen or heard, or believed, then how is the soul to be touched, the lesson learned?

REFERENCES

Blake, R. A. (2000). *After Image: The Indelible Catholic Imagination of Six American Filmmakers*. Chicago, IL; Loyola Press.

Lawton, R. B., (2003). The modern Catholic university: "How far from Eden?" In M. K. McCullough (Ed.), *Fire and Ice: Imagination and Intellect in the Catholic Tradition* (pp. 89–93). Scranton, PA: University of Scranton Press.

Searle, M. (1991). "Liturgy as metaphor." *Worship, 55*, 98–120.

Willcock, M. M. (Ed.). (1990). *Soliloquies: And Immortality of the Soul* (G. Watson, Trans.). Warminster, England: Aris & Phillips.

Computer Science, Community, and Faith

Stephanie E. August

H ow does faith fit into computer science curriculum? How are the fire of our imagination and the ice of our intellect tempered by our experience at a Catholic university? How are the Catholic customs, rituals, and sense of inclusion, along with the pursuit of inquiry, social justice, and connectedness, expressed by the way we live in the world, our everyday routine on campus, and, especially, the way we teach? The President's Institute on the Catholic Character of Loyola Marymount University gave faculty an opportunity to consider how to keep the Catholic faith at the center of teaching, scholarship, and service, yet satisfy the need to prepare students for careers in their chosen disciplines. Robert Bellah's (2003) concerns about the plight of Catholic education in America, the discussion raised by Doris Donnelly (2003) on the Catholic sacramental imagination, and testaments of others to the presence of God in their lives presented at the Institute provide a framework for identifying expressions of Catholicity in many aspects of campus activities as well as in the teaching of liberal arts courses. Yet my dry, concrete, technical field of computer science seems to lack opportunities for expressing faith.

The experience of the Institute challenged me to reconsider my view of the Church's presence in my own department and discipline, the way my faith affects my interactions with students, and ultimately the way commitment to mission transforms and influences my approach to teaching computer science. I found that we computer scientists do have ample opportunity to give witness to our beliefs as we interact with students, although it is rare for us to explicitly discuss faith as we teach. We are able to build community, balance imagination and intellect, and acknowledge our sources of insight. We can increase our effectiveness in this regard by becoming more involved in our students' extracurricular activities.

Catholic Education Builds Community

When students or faculty move from campus life to city life, they take with them an attitude toward the world and an ability to bring Catholic spirituality into secular activities which in turn engenders a Catholic identity. Outward signs of Catholicism are clearly present on campus in community celebrations of the Mass, in the Confirmation ceremony, and in the presence of the Marymount sisters and other sisters and the Jesuits and other priests. These are powerful symbols of shared Catholic beliefs and institutions. Yet even non-religious campus activities integrate Catholic attitudes and expose those who consciously avoid contact with anything explicitly Catholic to the university's mission. For example, the Marymount and Jesuit educational experience, which makes religious activities foundational, instills in its participants the need to view each individual as an integral part of a complete community and compels all participants to improve their world, especially through their professional lives. It is the sense of belonging to a unique and welcoming community that spreads beyond the campus to transform lives.

A goal of Catholic education is to recognize the presence of God in all things, and specifically in all parts of the educational experience. God's presence is most obvious in the fire of the experience, in an individual's interests, teaching style, activities, or community involvement. Its presence in the ice of practical job skills training and the content of courses may be less apparent. It is the responsibility of believing faculty to model faith to students, thus helping them recognize God's presence in their lives and their educational experience.

There is a tendency among computer scientists to view ourselves as somehow existing apart from the community, exempt from the norms of social behavior and interaction. Yet what we do is intimately integrated with every aspect of daily life, from communication (cell phones, the Internet) to health (patient monitoring systems) to space exploration (guidance systems); our success depends upon our ability to maintain ties to the community.

As a faculty we can increase community by attending student award ceremonies, barbeques, and banquets. In the gospel, Jesus used meals shared with friends as opportunities for persuading others to follow his example. At these events we can acknowledge the accomplishments of our students, as well as meet and acknowledge the support of spouses, parents, children, and friends who form each student's personal community. The fact that we are able to focus on minute details for hours on end in order to solve a problem does not excuse us from stepping back, looking at, and interacting with the larger world that uses our products and produces our developers.

Computer labs can also nurture a sense of community. As faculty, we need to cultivate concern for newcomers, rather than expecting them to fend for themselves, just as the mustard seed in the gospel needs to be cultivated to be productive. A computer lab can be an intimidating, alienating environment to a new student or faculty member. The newcomer must obtain a username and password before using any of the equipment, which usually requires identifying an unfamiliar lab assistant among a sea of unfamiliar faces. Then he/she needs to ascertain which machines run the software needed. This is not an easy task when the information is not posted or publicly available and again requires interfacing with strangers. Finally, the student needs to learn how to start up and use the software. People without "techie" backgrounds can be quickly put off by such a hostile environment and be lost to the field. As a result, we sometimes find ourselves isolated socially. We can increase a sense of community and social awareness in the labs by encouraging lab assistants to actively seek out students or faculty new to the lab and in need of assistance, rather than putting the burden on newcomers to make their needs known.

We are Called to Balance Imagination and Intellect

In her Institute address, Doris Donnelly (2003) notes that ". . . what often helps the eventual progressive disclosure of sacramental symbolism is familiarity with the world outside the official religious sphere—for example, in the arts—in poetry, music, and painting—in subjects we teach, in issues we raise in the classroom, and the discoveries we make there as well" (p. 52-53). Even in the dry, objective world of computer science, there is ample opportunity to observe God's presence in the world and impart moral values as faculty teach automata theory, programming languages, software engineering, and Internet technologies.

Robert Bellah (2003) expresses this concern. In a world of consumers, consumer students now make decisions, for better or for worse, that were once made by faculty. Bellah fears that by allowing students to drive the curriculum, the university is losing the ability to retain the breadth of studies that students need, in the long run, to succeed in the world. Our computer science, software engineering, and multimedia courses provide opportunities for faculty to increase students' breadth of knowledge, while allowing students to direct the curriculum in a limited, career-directed fashion.

In many technology courses, faculty choose the principles or problem-solving skills that the students need to learn, while the students often select the problem or domain to be investigated. This balances the students' need to gain the technical skills necessary to obtain jobs upon graduation (the intellect) with their desire to work on problems that are interesting and relevant to their lives (the imagination). For example, students in software engineering courses have an overwhelming tendency to implement computer games in both group and individual projects. Rather than be dismayed by what appears on the surface to be a rather limited domain, it is in fact an opportunity to explore various problem-solving strategies and systems integration issues. Students struggle to build on their basic knowledge of operating systems, networking, graphics, algorithms, artificial intelligence, and database management systems to produce their final product. Outsiders attending the end-of-semester demonstrations might simply see yet another implementation of Pac Man or another shoot-em-up game that appeals to adolescent star-fighter wannabe's. However, a deeper look reveals a complete and intense effort to integrate multiple difficult tasks and present the project as a polished masterpiece, requiring a tenuous balance of imagination and intellect. The students drive the selection of the problem to be studied: it is the responsibility of the faculty to see that basic principles and problem-solving skills of the discipline are employed.

In the Catholic university setting, we live and work in an internet-based, multimedia world. Students ask for opportunities to learn how to incorporate various media into the systems they are building. A multimedia course uses a different strategy to respond to the students' needs. Here, the students are given the task of designing and developing a multimedia presentation, to be used by a department on campus. For example, one year the students produced a compact disk introducing the university to new students. This CD was later distributed to all incoming freshmen. In this case, the students specified the principles, and the faculty provided the problem to be solved. This two-semester course has the added benefit of being an interdisciplinary effort. It draws students majoring in communication and fine arts, history, English, or mathematics, as well as computer science. It provides an excellent opportunity for non-technical majors to become more familiar with information systems that they will undoubtedly encounter as they venture out into the world after graduation. The course also provides the computer science majors an opportunity to learn to work with and appreciate the contributions of students from other disciplines. The balance of the imagination and intellect are found in learning environments such as this, where the fire of the imagination runs free, while the ice of academic discipline guides the effort.

Grace in Our Work

The Catholic imagination is about seeing God in everyday things. One might think it difficult to find God in the banal logic of a computer program. How can a person possibly have a spiritual experience by studying the scope of a variable, or tracking down a missing semicolon? Just as Brian Doyle (1999), writing in *Notre Dame Magazine*, speaks of experiencing ". . . the deft grace of the doctors who edited" (p. 49) his son's defective heart, computer programmers can be filled with grace as they mend code. The diseases the programmers diagnose are typically errors previously made in the design or implementation of computer programs. Repairing these programs is an error prone process. One "bug fix" can easily result in the inclusion of ten additional bugs or errors into a program. With this in mind, computer scientists must approach programming with both the wisdom that comes from being well versed in their craft and the grace that flows from the benevolent being that guides their actions and leads them to a more perfect world.

It is not enough, in the field of computer science, to be able to write a good piece of stand-alone code. As Bellah (2003) points out, a true scholar is not only knowledgeable or skillful, but also has qualities of character and an ethical stance toward the world. Computer scientists must always be aware of how each piece of a complete system integrates with the others and how it relates to the overall quality of the product under development. Students must learn the published ethics of their profession and understand why these professional ethics exist. John Motil (1979), a computer science professor at Cal State Northridge, insists on this from day one. He includes the following examination of conscience in his text on programming principles:

So your program works . . . but
working is not sufficient!
    Is it easy to read and understand?
    Is it easy to describe or explain?
    Is it easy to improve or optimize?
    Is it easy to code (implement) and document?
    Is it easy to test or debug?
    Is it easy to extend or modify?
    Is it easy to analyze and evaluate?
    Is it easy to prove? (p. C-1)

This simple checklist became an integral part of my teaching. I can help my students grow in terms of moral conscience by giving them "prayers" like this, and exposing them to the published ethics of the Association for Computing Machinery, which is readily available on the Internet. I do not teach my students that the occurrence of disasters, such as the failure of a mission to Mars, a space shuttle explosion, an improperly ground Hubble telescope lens, and the disintegration of a jet off the coast of California can be prevented, but that they will be much less likely to occur if corporations do engineering with a conscience. Developing a conscience in the computer industry means always looking beyond the immediate project responsibilities, to the quality of the overall product, always insisting that the highest standards be met.

In the college curriculum, the final opportunity to present and discuss these issues of ethics is in senior year, when the students work on both individual and group software projects in the software engineering and senior-project lab courses. The projects are self-directed and intended to give the students a chance to demonstrate the depth of their abilities, as well as to convey basic software engineering principles. These principles must include not only how to produce a working product that meets written requirements, but also how to produce one that is documented and easy to maintain. It is interesting to note that the ethics of the computer science profession include standards for relating to colleagues, as well as for developing an excellent product. In these courses, the students' responsibilities are twofold: They must complete their own projects, and they must review and critique the work of the other students. This arrangement simulates the experience they will have in the workplace following graduation. The students soon learn that there is more to completing a project than simply writing code. They must depend upon each other, and they soon learn that the projects run much more smoothly if they follow the engineering principles they have already learned and relate to one another with responsibility, respect, and trust. Faculty encourages students to engage in constructive criticism and be guided by respect in all interactions with their peers. Addressing the interpersonal problems that inevitably arise provides the faculty another occasion to reinforce the moral values that are a fundamental part of the Catholic belief system—each individual is valued, each is able to and expected to make a contribution to the overall effort, and each deserves respect at all times.

Beyond fostering community and beyond integrating imagination and intellect, Catholic education by its very nature seeks to instill connectedness. How can students in a Catholic university become and remain connected to their church, their colleagues, the university, and their profession? How can the spirit of connection help the students to transform their communities beyond the university? Connectedness to a faith community can grow from the example set by faculty and the availability of spiritual experiences on campus. Faculty can encourage students to remain in touch with their colleagues and with the values of the university by sponsoring, supporting, and attending student events.

In the final analysis, it is not just the fire of imagination or the ice of intellect, it is the way the two work in communion with each other that is the essence of Catholic education. Asking questions, never being satisfied that an answer has been totally revealed, seeking a better answer, a better solution, a better way of life, and more perfect connections is the goal of Catholic education. Catholic education is seeking God's kingdom in all we do here on earth.

REFERENCES

Bellah, R. N. (2003). "On being Catholic and American." In M. K. McCullough (Ed.), *Fire and Ice: Imagination and Intellect in the Catholic Tradition* (pp.31–48). Scranton, PA: University of Scranton Press.

Donnelly, D. (2003). "The Catholic Sacramental Imagination." In M. K. McCullough (Ed.), *Fire and Ice: Imagination and Intellect in the Catholic Tradition* (pp.49–66). Scranton, PA: University of Scranton Press.

Doyle, B. (1999, Autumn). "Filled with grace." *Notre Dame Magazine*, 46–49.

Motil, J. (1979). *Programming Principles*. Reseda, CA: Ridgeview Publishing Company.

A Twenty-first Century Challenge:
Hiring for Mission in Catholic Higher Education

Michael P. Geis

T hroughout the United States today, Catholic colleges and universities are engaged in a complex and challenging task as they attempt to improve their standing in the national community of higher education, even while protecting their religious heritage.

These universities are opening their doors to an increasingly diverse range of students, recruiting excellent scholars in all disciplines, promoting competitive research, and also trying to retain their Catholic religious character. A major concern in maintaining a clearly visible and robust Catholic presence is the steadily declining number of religious, who traditionally populated these Catholic campuses and were the public face of the church in these schools. Further, as many outstanding opportunities for Catholic students have opened in secular and other private universities, and as Catholic students have become more mobile, it has become ever more imperative that Catholic colleges and universities compete for excellent students of many religious traditions. Situated in one of the nation's most dynamic, diverse, and rapidly changing geographical regions, Loyola Marymount University in Los Angeles is, at least in several significant ways, a revealing example of such an institution.

The University's Mission in Its Early History

Michael Engh, S.J., (2000, 2003) a member of LMU's History Department, provided Institute participants with an interpretive history of the University, tracing its background from the founding of both Loyola University of Los Angeles and Marymount College. The picture that emerges from that history is consistent with the general development of Catholic higher education in the United States. It is well documented that, by and large, Catholics were viewed with considerable suspicion by the Protestant leadership in the early period of

157

the United States and were (with exceptions) generally unwelcome in government, business, and education. Institutions of higher education founded and operated by Catholics (usually from Europe) thus provided unique opportunities for Catholics to attain the educational level that leadership requires in society. These schools simultaneously maintained a strong religious presence and fostered an active faith among their students. Another benefit they offered was the formation of strong social bonds among future Catholic leaders—bonds that could and did lead to the creation of a Catholic infrastructure in commerce in this country. These were vitally important characteristics of Catholic higher education through a long era, when most Catholics had few prospects of advancement within the educational establishment in the broader society. This state of affairs extended into the 20th century.

Although the picture significantly changed by the 1960s, when I was an undergraduate, it is nevertheless interesting to consider the way in which Loyola University of Los Angeles expressed its educational mission at that time. The following excerpts from the *Loyola University Bulletin* for the 1962-63 academic year are illustrative. (Keep in mind that Loyola and Marymount had not yet merged; that the university was not yet coeducational.)

> The educational system in use at Loyola is . . . the same as that employed in the many colleges and universities conducted by the Society of Jesus in nearly all parts of the world.

> In its moral training, the University directs its efforts toward developing the moral judgment of its students for the right fulfillment of their civil and religious duties. The avowed purpose of its training is to lay a solid foundation in the mind and character of the student, sufficient for any superstructure of science and arts and letters; fully adequate, too, for the upbuilding of that moral life, civil and religious, which must ever be rated the highest and truest honor of worthy manhood.

> Knowledge and intellectual development of themselves have no moral efficacy whatever; science, as such, has never made one true man. . . . Religion alone can purify the heart and guide and strengthen the will. Religion alone can

furnish the solid basis upon which high ideals of business integrity and moral cleanliness will be fostered and conserved. Religious truth, then, must be the very atmosphere that the student breathes. Christianity must suffuse with its light all that he reads, illuminating what is noble and exposing what is base, giving to the true and to the false their relative light and shade. The divine truths and principles of consistent Christianity must needs be the vital force animating the whole organic structure of education. Accordingly, the study of theology is prescribed for all Catholic students. (*Bulletin*, Loyola University of Los Angeles, 1962, p. 32)

The *Bulletin* statement continues with a description of "The Loyola Man," concluding with the following claim:

Loyola aims to train a man for success and for possible greatness; but whatever a man's worldly achievement, Loyola's training insists that his design of living include the fulfillment of his obligations toward God and his own soul and prepare him thus to be, in the best sense, a Complete Man, a Citizen of Two Worlds. (*Bulletin*, Loyola University of Los Angeles, 1962, p. 33)

It is probably fair to claim that, although the language chosen today is surely more conversational and less didactic and stilted, a number of LMU faculty would subscribe at least to the spirit of these statements. But certainly the phrasing of the mission of LMU is now less explicitly religious in its tone.

Changing Times, Unchanged Mission

The social conditions that surrounded the founding of most Jesuit, and other Catholic universities and colleges, have obviously changed enormously. But one specific and important change is that Catholic students are now welcome at all state-sponsored schools around the country, and even at many religiously oriented private schools. (For example, at California Lutheran University, one administrator said recently that while the student body was predominantly Lutheran in the early years of the school's existence, now Catholics outnumber Lutheran students, and have become the largest single religious group on that campus.) In the meantime, Jesuit and other Catholic colleges and universities have welcomed a wide range of backgrounds in their students, and have seen a steady increase in the fraction of their student populations who are not Catholics. Dr. Joseph Jabbra, LMU's Academic Vice President, recently reported to the Faculty Senate that as of fall, 2000, some 59% of LMU undergraduates were identified as Catholic. This figure represents a decline that has occurred over several decades. In the 1960s, the corresponding value was roughly 80%. (Jabbra, personal interview, 2001).

Understandably, as Catholic colleges and universities have lost a type of automatic advantage in enrolling Catholic students, and have strengthened their appeal to a broader cross-section of students from many faiths (or none), the articulation of these institutions' missions has changed, although, in the most fundamental sense, it is compatible with the earlier mission statements. For example, the LMU undergraduate *Bulletin* for 2000-2001, in its statement of History and Goals, proclaims that the University's Board of Trustees ". . . recognized the riches of a variety of religious traditions represented among the dedicated faculty and staff that complemented and enhanced the school's heritage of Catholic values." The florid language of the 1960s era bulletin is replaced by the statement that:

> Loyola Marymount understands and declares its purpose to be: The Encouragement of Learning, The Education of the Whole Person, The Service of Faith and the Promotion of Justice. (*Bulletin*, Loyola Marymount University, 2000, p. 9)

Similarly, the following statement is also found in the LMU *Mission, Goals, and Objectives* booklet of 1990:

> Loyola Marymount University: Promotes Academic Excellence; Provides a Liberal Education; Fosters a Student-centered University; Creates a Sense of Community on Campus; Participates Actively in the Life of the Larger Community; Lives an Institutional Commitment to Roman Catholicism and the Judeo-Christian Tradition. (*Loyola Marymount University Mission, Goals, and Objectives*, 1990)

Has the mission of the University changed over these 40 years? In the most fundamental sense, the best answer is that it has not. Then and now, the mission and goals of LMU and similar Catholic institutions have consistently committed them to provide a quality education and to prepare men and women of conscience, moral commitment, and religious faith (Engh, 2003).

Nonetheless, there has been enough significant change to force Catholic universities to give serious thought to what they are and what they are becoming. The focus of their mission is less explicit, less insistent on molding Catholic leaders, and more on a broader, more universal (and presumably more modern) person of conscience, somehow inspired by a Catholic and Judeo-Christian tradition. Clearly, the latter-day version of the mission is better suited to the broad range of religious backgrounds of current students and clearly more amenable to the more cosmopolitan, less parochial institutions of today. But there can be little wonder that, increasingly, members of university communities are asking questions like, "In what ways are we a Catholic school?" and "What is the role of Catholicism at our Catholic colleges and universities?"

Exploring The Nature of the Modern Jesuit University

Following a national gathering at Georgetown University in 1989 of Jesuits and their coworkers in higher education, a number of persons from various Jesuit universities in the United States met at Creighton University in Omaha. They included both religious and lay administrators and faculty; their purpose was to open a discussion of the future of Catholic higher education. Specifically, they wished to explore possibilities for maintaining the Jesuit and Catholic nature of their universities in an era of decreasing numbers of Jesuits. Lacking a better name for themselves, they dubbed their meeting "Collaboration in Mission." Because the conversation in Omaha seemed fruitful, other such conferences were subsequently held, at St. Louis University in 1990, Loyola University of New Orleans in 1991, and Gonzaga University in Spokane in 1992. I was fortunate to be able to participate in the last three.

At the 1990 meeting, Dr. Alice B. Hayes, Executive Vice President at St. Louis University (the host school), addressed the participants, raising the question of what features of Jesuit education they should strive to preserve. She cited a recent Loyola University of Chicago survey on this topic. While those who conducted the survey hoped to see such suggestions as intellectual rigor, moral formation, and commitment to faith and justice, the respondents' dominant answer was "the presence of Jesuits," including a Jesuit president. Not very encouraging news for a group concerned about how to maintain the Jesuit character of an institution in face of a diminishing number of Jesuits!

Gradually, however, as the series of conferences ran its course, the *de facto* conclusion became apparent: that a "critical mass" (not easily defined) of lay faculty sympathetic to the history and nature of Jesuit/Catholic schools was essential for maintaining their distinguishing intellectual, ethical, and religious characteristics. But the implication that recruiting sympathetic faculty and staff should become a priority in the hiring process produced some uncomfortably sharp exchanges at the final meeting at Gonzaga in 1992. Many came away with the impression that people had found their way to an insight, even a conclusion, but were not sure where to go with it.

If practical strategies for recruiting and hiring for mission were not immediately apparent, it was nonetheless clear that programs to inculturate new faculty, and to deepen the understanding of the Jesuit/Catholic character of the schools on the part of ongoing faculty, were also crucial. Individual campuses addressed these needs in various ways—orientation days, retreats, summer seminars, etc. In addition, several regional groupings of Jesuit universities were organized to bring together faculty (and in some cases faculty and staff) to share common concerns and to continue the conversation about how to preserve the special nature of their academic communities.

A Twenty-first Century Challenge

Any effort to maintain and develop the religious character of Jesuit and other Catholic universities depends upon people. No matter what is written in a mission and goals statement or an undergraduate bulletin, committed individuals must be present in sufficient numbers to make the religious character a lived reality. Faculty, administrators, staff, and students all have a role to play, but in the view of many the premier challenge, as recognized at Gonzaga in 1992, is to hire faculty for mission.

Hiring for mission does *not* mean hiring only Catholics, but it does mean recruiting and hiring practices that lead to a significant number of faculty who will find ways to promote the values and goals of the Jesuit/Catholic university.

While many faculty members in Catholic and other church-related colleges and universities struggle with the question of hiring for mission, others oppose any effort to introduce into the recruitment process factors outside of the fundamental effort to attract the best qualified research scholars and teachers. But if no effort is made to assure that new faculty are committed to the promotion of the university's traditions and goals, it is likely that over time the collective commitment will be lost. Too many once religiously affiliated colleges and universities, that have now become secular, testify to this danger.

The Lilly Network of Church-Related Colleges and Universities recently provided support for faculty from four of its member institutions in Southern California to meet and share their concerns over their schools' future. The participating schools were California Lutheran University, Pepperdine University, Westmont College, and Loyola Marymount University. At the gathering on the Pepperdine campus in Malibu, it became clear that Pepperdine (affiliated with the Church of Christ) is engaged in a conscious effort to attract and recruit faculty who are interested in its faith commitment and are supportive of its institutional goals. (Incidentally, two speakers at that meeting were Catholic members of Pepperdine's faculty, pointing out again that hiring for mission does not necessarily mean hiring from only a specific religious denomination.) Efforts to hire for mission will doubtless vary from one institution to another, and practices that seem desirable at one school may be unacceptable at another. But this is an issue that surely cannot be ignored. It is a key challenge that Catholic colleges and universities in the United States must confront.

In his Institute presentation, Dr. Robert Bellah (2003) made this challenge to Catholic universities explicit when he expressed his belief "that this is a Catholic moment in American cultural history." He discussed at some length the dialectical and analogical approaches to truth—the former more Protestant with its emphasis on word and the latter more Catholic in its kinship with sacramentality—and concluded (I will not attempt to reconstruct his argument) that at the present time. Protestants and Catholics alike badly need an infusion of the analogical imagination to help us overcome the cultural confusion into which we have fallen. Bellah (2003) cited Alasdair MacIntyre and Charles Taylor, both accomplished philosophers, with interests also in the social sciences, history, and theology, as examples of Catholic scholars who might serve as admirable role models for the kind of faculty members who could make a university with a Catholic identity become a reality today.

Bellah was quick to acknowledge, however, that it will not be easy for Catholic universities to find scholars of the caliber of MacIntyre and Taylor; and that when such scholars do emerge, they may need to be recruited as "targets of opportunity." Even so, MacIntyre's and Taylor's concern for substance rooted in an intellectual tradition, as much as for critical thinking about that tradition, suggests some possible considerations for search committees at Catholic universities looking for faculty candidates with a good mission fit. For example, which candidates are able to affirm the possibility of knowing truth and the coherence of learning across department lines? Which candidates are open to the integration of faith and reason and the affirmation of values? Which candidates see their students' growth in virtue—including the virtues associated with building a just society—as a function of education?

Bellah may not have provided practical answers to all the vexing questions of hiring for mission, but his Institute presentation, for many who heard it, brought the discussion to a new level of urgency. It is imperative for Loyola Marymount and other Catholic universities, as they face diminishing numbers of religious faculty, to supplement their ranks with at least a few outstanding scholars who are able to integrate their academic lives with a vibrant Catholic faith. But even more generally, if the institutions are to remain true to their history, their lived heritage, and the ideals enshrined in their mission statements, they must find ways, in all their faculty recruiting, to attract and hire significant numbers of young professors—whether coreligionists or not—who are open to the riches of the Catholic intellectual and imaginative tradition as an alternative to value-free secular education. This is the challenge confronting Catholic higher education at the beginning of the 21st century.

REFERENCES

Bellah, R. N. (2003). "On being Catholic and American." In M. K. McCullough (Ed.), *Fire and Ice: Imagination and Intellect in the Catholic Tradition* (pp. 31–48). Scranton, PA: University of Scranton Press.

Engh, M. E., S.J. (2003). "The best sort of liberal education: A history of the intellectual tradition at Loyola Marymount University." In M. K. McCullough (Ed.), *Fire and Ice: Imagination and Intellect in the Catholic Tradition* (pp. 1–29). Scranton, PA: University of Scranton Press.

Engh, M. E., S.J. (2000). "Just ones past and present at Loyola Marymount University." In M. K. McCullough (Ed.), *The Just One Justices: The Role of Justice at the Heart of Catholic Higher Education* (pp. 21–36). Scranton, PA: University of Scranton Press.

Loyola Marymount University Bulletin (2000), 70, (2). Los Angeles, CA: Loyola University.

Loyola Marymount University (1990). Mission, goals, and objectives. Los Angeles, CA: Loyola Marymount University.

Loyola University of Los Angeles Bulletin (1962), 32, (1). Los Angeles, CA: Loyola University.

Contributors

Stephanie August, Ph.D., is an Assistant Professor in Computer Science and Electrical Engineering at Loyola Marymount University. She is also director of the Computer Science graduate programs.

Robert Bellah, Ph.D., is Professor Emeritus of the Sociology of Religion at the University of California, Berkeley. Beyond his academic discipline, Dr. Bellah is well known for *Habits of the Heart* (1985), *The Good Society* (1992), and many other books.

Richard Blake, S.J., Ph.D., is a Professor of Film Studies in the Fine Arts Department at Boston College. He serves as film critic for *America* magazine and is author of *Afterimage: The Indelible Catholic Imagination of Six American Filmmakers* (2000).

Robert Caro, S.J., Ph.D., is a Professor of English at Loyola Marymount University where he also serves as Assistant to the President for Mission and Identity. He was program coordinator for the 2000 President's Institute on the Catholic Character of LMU.

Doris Donnelly, Ph.D., is a Professor of Theology at John Carroll University, Cleveland. She serves as Director of the Cardinal Suenens Program in Theology and Church Life at John Carroll and is a frequent contributor to *Theology Today* and other journals.

Michael Engh, S.J., Ph.D., is an Associate Professor of History and Acting Dean of the College of Liberal Arts at Loyola Marymount University. His specialization is in the history of the American West, with an emphasis on religion and society. He has directed extensive student research on the history of LMU.

Michael Geis, Ph.D., is a Professor of Chemistry and Biochemistry at Loyola Marymount University. His research focuses on the three-dimensional structures of organic molecules. Dr. Geis has served as President of LMU's Faculty Senate.

Howard Lavick, M.F.A., Associate Professor of Film and Television at Loyola Marymount, is Acting Dean of the University's newly established School of Film and Television.

Robert Lawton, S.J., Ph.D., the 14th President of Loyola Marymount University, is a classicist and scripture scholar as well as an administrator. His current research is in the area of strategic planning and the Catholic tradition in education.

Sharon Locy, Ph.D., is a Professor of English and Director of the Liberal Studies Program at Loyola Marymount University. A specialist in 19th century British literature, she is currently working on the female *bildungsroman* in Victorian fiction.

Marie Anne Mayeski, Ph.D., Professor of Historical Theology at Loyola Marymount University, specializes in medieval theology. Her "New Voices in the Tradition: Medieval Hagiography Revisited" appeared in *Theological Studies* (December 2002).

Scott Wood, J.D., is an Associate Clinical Professor at Loyola Marymount University's downtown campus of Loyola Law School. He teaches legal writing, ethical lawyering, negotiation, and law and literature.

Poetry Contributors

Jane Crawford, Ph.D., Professor and Chair, Classics and Archaeology.

Sharon Locy, Ph.D., Professor, English.

Mladen Milicevic, Ph.D., Associate Professor, School of Film and Television.

Herbert Ryan, S.J., Professor, Theological Studies.

Scott Wood, J.D., Associate Clinical Professor, Loyola Law School.

Editor

Mary K. McCullough, Ph.D., is a Professor of Educational Administration in the School of Education at Loyola Marymount University. She is editor of a previous Institute volume, *The Just One*

Justices: The Role of Justice at the Heart of Catholic Higher Education (2000), University of Scranton Press.

Staff

Rebecca Herr, Research assistant and graduate student in the Master of Arts in Teaching program at Loyola Marymount University.

Annette Pijuan, M.A., Research assistant and Catholic high school mathematics teacher.

INDEX

S

Sacrament xv-xvi, 33, 49, 51-52, 113, 122
Sacramental Theology xi, 50-52
Searle, Mark 143, 145-146, 148
Sexton, Anne xii, 56-60, 66
Shakespeare 98, 104-111
Sisters of St. Joseph of Orange 14, 24
Soul xvi, xviii, 8-9, 26, 34-37, 39, 47, 57-58, 69-72, 114, 117, 136-138, 145, 147-148,
          159
St. Anselm of Canterbury 129
St. Louis University 161
Sullivan, Joseph, S.J. 8, 10, 42, 46
Suspension of Disbelief 143, 146
Swidler, Ann 42, 46, 98

T

Taylor, Charles xi, 31, 38-43, 47, 164
Tracy, David xi, 32, 34, 40, 47, 51, 66, 72, 87

U

University of Chicago 35, 46-47

V

Vatican II xi, 12, 18, 22, 29, 38, 51-52
Vietnam War 72, 77, 85

W

Welles, Orson 145
Westmont College 163
Wood, Scott vii, xiv-xv, xix, 10, 63, 97, 168